the herman miller collection 1952

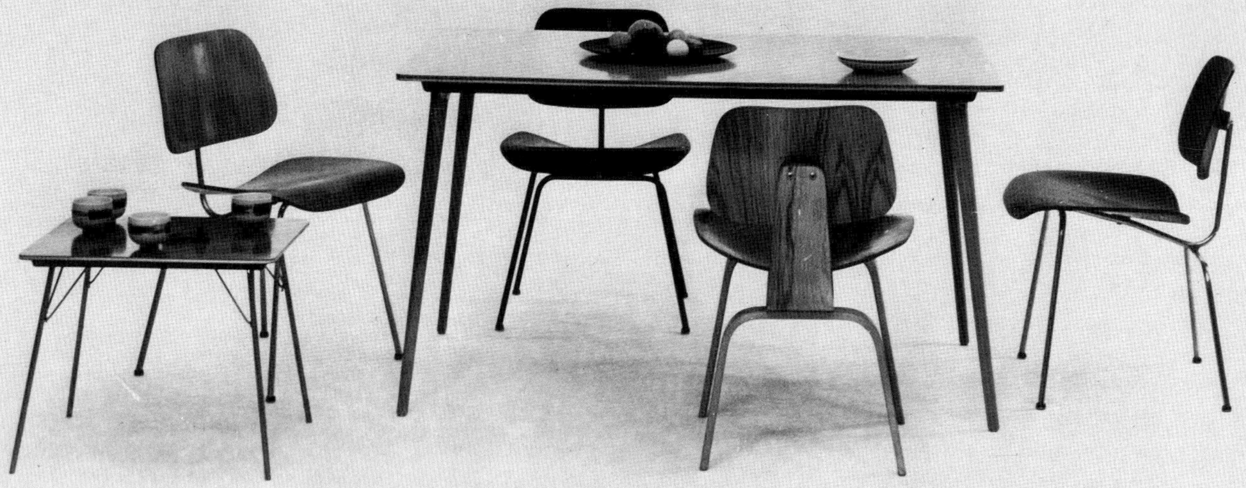

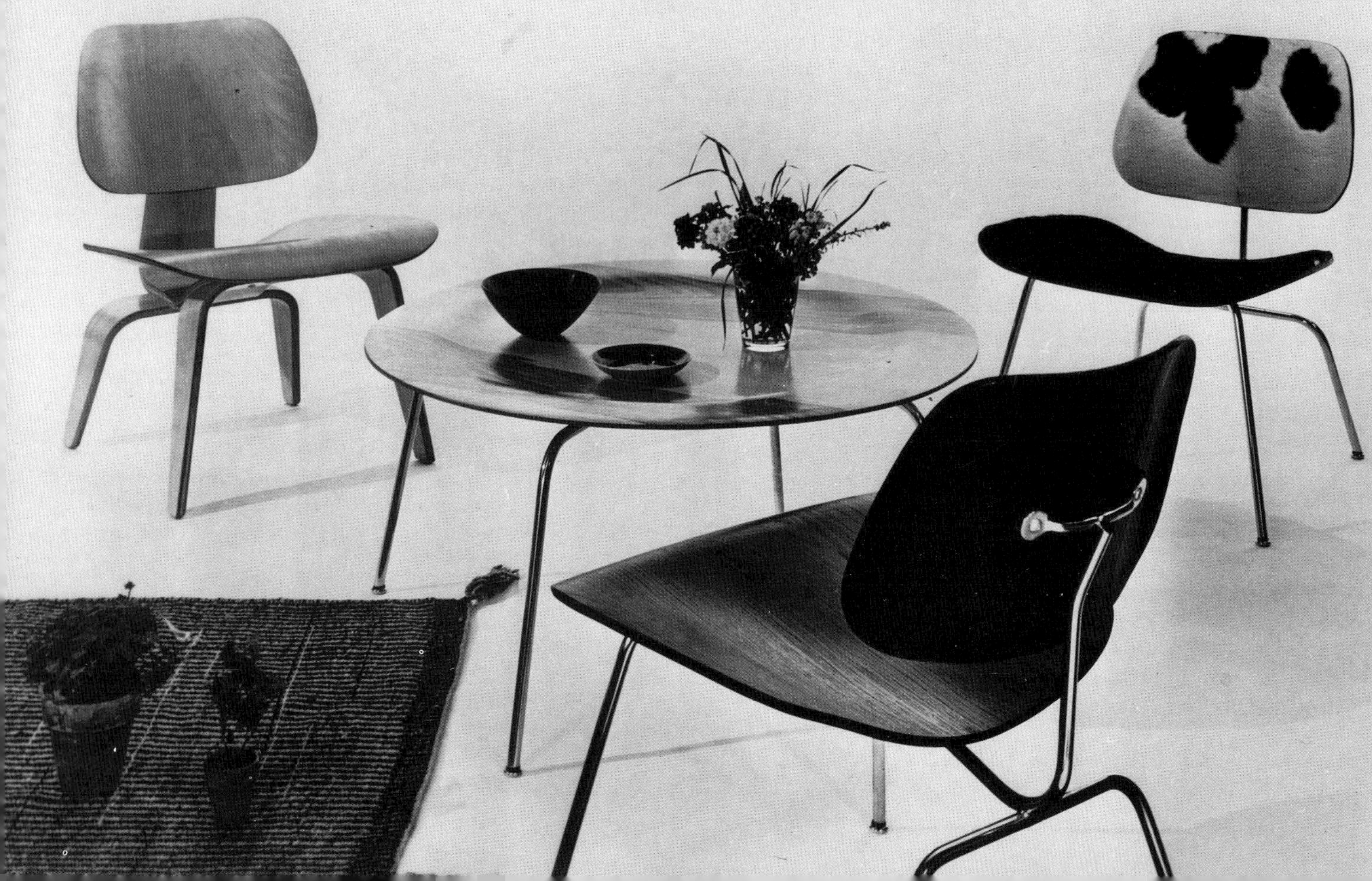

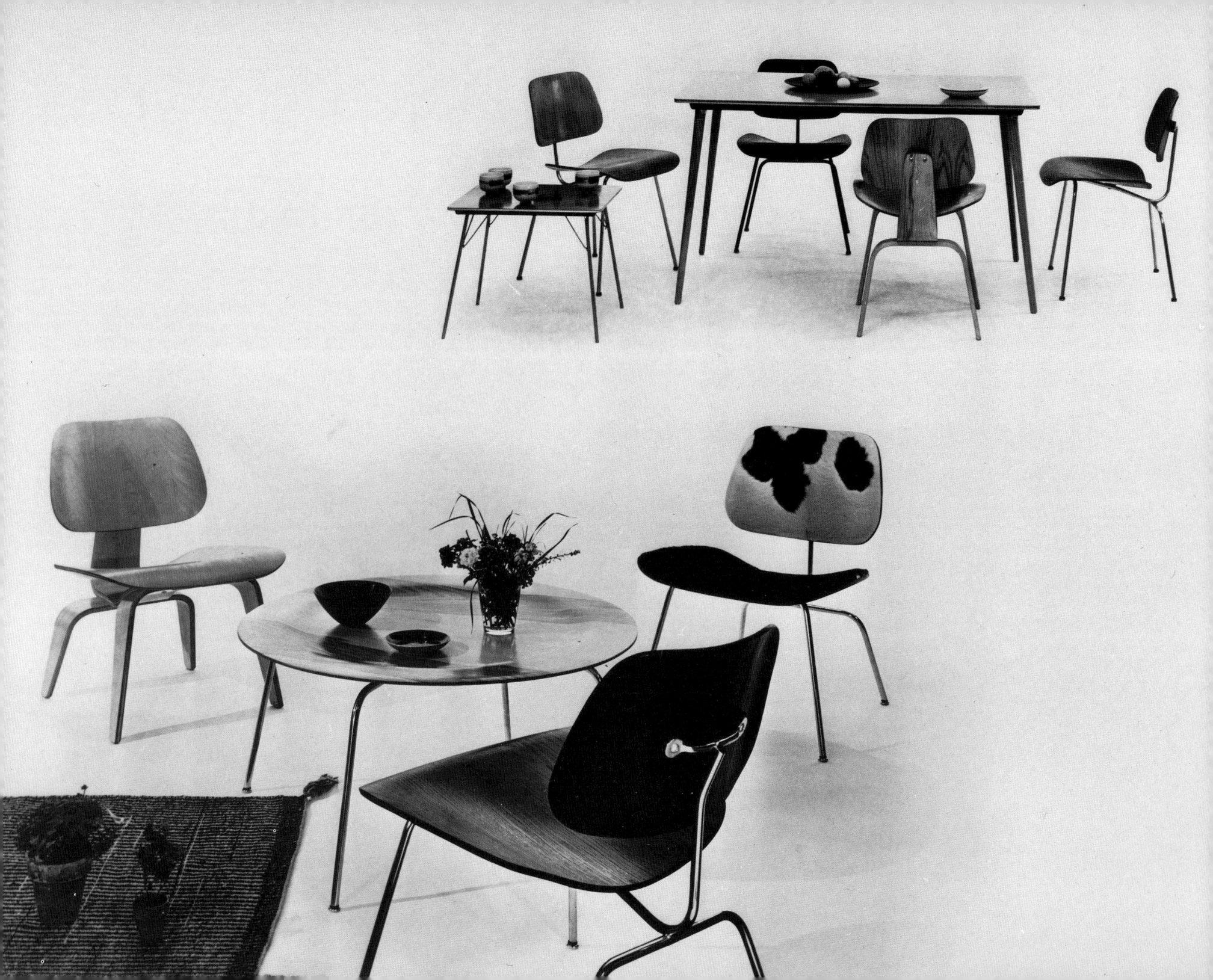

ACANTHUS PRESS REPRINT SERIES
THE 20TH CENTURY: LANDMARKS IN DESIGN
VOLUME **5**

Furniture designed by
George Nelson and Charles Eames,
with occasional pieces by
Isamu Noguchi, Peter Hvidt and O.M. Nielsen.
With a new introduction by Ralph Caplan.

the herman miller collection 1952

ACANTHUS PRESS, NEW YORK 1995

Published by Acanthus Press
Barry Cenower, Publisher
54 West 21st Street
New York, New York 10010
(212) 463-0750

Library of Congress Cataloging–in–Publication Data

Herman Miller (Firm)
The Herman Miller collection 1952: furniture designed by George Nelson and Charles Eames, with occasional pieces by Isamu Noguchi, Peter Hvidt, and O.M. Nielsen / with a new introduction by Ralph Caplan.
   p.   cm. — (Acanthus Press reprint series. The 20th century, landmarks in design; v. 5)
Originally published: Zeeland, Mich.: Herman Miller, 1952.
ISBN 0–926494–05–8 : $37.50
1. Herman Miller (Firm) — Catalogs.   2. Furniture — United States — History — 20th century — Catalogs.   3. Nelson, George, 1908–   .
4. Eames, Charles. I. Title. II. Series: Acanthus Press reprint series. 20th century, landmarks in design; v. 5.
NK2439.H42A4   1995
684.1'0029'477415—dc20

94–45982
CIP

Printed in the USA

introduction

Several years ago I was in the Grand Rapids Art Museum for the opening of a traveling exhibition of furniture. A television crew was on hand and asked me to comment on, and in, the Eames molded plywood chair. I sat down and cleared my throat for on–camera pontification when a very young and very indignant curator stormed into the room.

"You can't sit on that!" he cried. "That is an art object on loan from the Smithsonian Institute."

"It's the Smithsonian Institution," I snidely corrected. "And this particular art object is produced in a factory 30 miles down the road by people who make it specifically for sitting in. They think it's furniture." Several variations of the object in question appear on page 93. I think it's furniture too, but of a splendor that understandably confuses curators. They think it is art. I, on the other hand, may be similarly confused by this catalog. There are moments when I think *it* is art. Yet, no matter how our hearts soar at the prospect of its being in print again, this volume is, after all, a tool manufactured for the quotidian task of selling furniture and, as such, has only modest claims to literary stature.

There are precedents of course. Early editions of both the Sears and Montgomery Ward catalogs have been reissued as trade books. They induce an agreeable nostalgia, and they illuminate social history as few documents can. The present volume, I suppose, does both those things too, although any sense of nostalgia is diminished by the number of these products that are still, or once more, in the Herman Miller line or roughly depicted in hundreds of knockoffs. That is only one aspect of the book's stunning contemporary validity. Although some of the other products are dated, the principles of their design are still being discovered and announced daily. (For that matter, the dated products don't stay dated: day beds are now being rediscovered as excellent alternatives to the various convertibles and futons that once replaced them.)

There are other striking points of contemporaneity. Certain themes and concerns appear throughout the book as if they were minted yesterday. Anyone familiar with the buzzwords and buzzbooks of corporate America in the nineties will find here more than a hint of the "search for excellence," "quality circles" (in this case, a quality triangle consisting of maker, designer, customer), "the reinvented corporation," and "user centered design." And, at a time when newspapers and magazines regularly feature articles on the home office as a design challenge peculiar to the electronic nineties, it is interesting to see how seriously designers were thinking about it in the forties. To describe a desk as "a fine working instrument" presages Bruce Burdick's 1980 "Beam." And the characterization of the executive office as "a daytime living room where work can be done under less tension with fewer distractions" might come from next month's in-flight magazine.

For all its air of timeliness, however, this book is deliciously old-fashioned in its literacy. Its author, George Nelson, was to become celebrated as much for his writing as for his design, and his clean prose, like the clean lines of the furniture he is writing about, exemplifies a freedom from pretentiousness rare in design writing and in design. Without pretending to be anything that it is not, without in fact pretending to be anything at all, the catalog is a practical reference for anyone who cares about the design imperative.

The catalog—the second edition of the one published in 1948—represents a unique small company at the threshold of becoming a large one. By 1952 Herman Miller, George Nelson, and Charles Eames were all much better known than they had been even four years earlier. The times were confident. More than a million veterans had entered college on the GI Bill of Rights. In 1948 Peter Goldmark invented the long-playing record, creating the need for new cabinetry to house record players and the television picture tubes that were already poised for ubiquity. Manufacturers were eager to exploit new technologies. Materials unavailable during the war years were available again and, moreover, they were being supplanted by new ones. Plastics, initially perceived as cheap substitutes for more expensive materials, were reinterpreted as prestige commodities. The same Formica that was practical in dinettes became positively sophisticated in coffee tables.

Designers were among the first to take an egalitarian view of materials, welcoming new ones, as those who truly love the past invariably do. In 1940 Eero Saarinen and Charles Eames came to public attention with a plywood shell chair covered with foam rubber. It won first prize in The Museum of Modern Art's influential "Organic Designs in Home Furnishings" exhibition, initiated by the architect Eliot Noyes, who headed the museum's department of industrial design. At the time this catalog was published, Saarinen had already begun work on his famous pedestal chair, in the belief that "great furniture of the past has been a structural total" and that the totality could be achieved in reinforced plastic. Since it wasn't, he coated the cast aluminum base with plastic so the chair looked unified.

The idea of Modern—the idea that an artifact ought to express the times in which it was made—was itself modern. Traditionally, it had meant something quite different. *The Manual of the Furniture Arts and Crafts*, published in Grand Rapids in 1928, explained, "To define modern furniture, that is, the furniture which has been in popular use within the past five years, would require a rehearsal of practically all known periods and styles. At no time in the history of furniture has there been a more general use of all schools known to the furniture arts."

Modern, in other words, meant contemporary in manufacture but meant nothing at all in respect to style. In 1942 Herman Miller's first design director, Gilbert Rohde, issued an amusing brochure "History of Modern Furniture," making the point that any good original work at any given time was modern. Designers (like poets and painters) take for granted that all periods are modern at the time we're living through them. Not until "modern times" did Modern become a period unto itself.

But the industry and the market were more comfortable with distant periods. Spanish Colonial had a strong appeal to people who were not Spaniards and did not live in colonies. "American" furniture was Early American.

"Grand Rapids furniture" betokened a general uncertainty in taste. It is easy for us today to feel superior to period copies, although Postmodernism has made it somewhat harder. Yet their success was rooted in the same longing for assured taste that a few years later helped make Scandinavian Contemporary so widely successful. It offered a reliable answer to the question: How can we be sure it's good? You could be sure because tastemakers said it was. It looked both familiar and acceptably foreign. By 1949, when The Museum of Modern Art began to label products as "good design," the security blanket of established taste was already being woven by magazines, advertising agencies, department stores, and others identified as "the tastemakers" by Russell Lynes, in his popular book of that name.

The Herman Miller company had something of a head start in developing a modern perspective. In 1930, when the company was making undistinguished period reproductions, the designer Gilbert Rohde walked unannounced into their Grand Rapids showroom with a mission. He was relatively new to the furniture industry, where manufacturer's staff designers sat at tables piled high with period books from which they took their inspiration and their four seasonal lines. To an extent almost unimaginable now, design in the industry meant copying. Good design in the industry meant copying well.

But Rohde was urging design that did not ignore the time in which it was made but identified with it, even exulted in it. While it is doubtful that he ever used the term "alternate lifestyles," this in fact is what he talked about to founder and CEO D.J. De Pree. Families were getting smaller, Rohde argued.

Houses were getting smaller too, with lower ceilings. People in cities were living in apartments that could not accommodate traditional furniture, either spatially or aesthetically. Also, values were changing. Respectability and worth were no longer expressed by bulk and weight or by ornate carving. There was a new simplicity, a new honesty.

De Pree listened carefully. Simplicity to a Grand Rapids manufacturer seemed a little strange, but honesty he could understand. He knew, and candidly said he knew, very little about design and virtually nothing about modern design, but he knew a great deal about honesty. In his foreword to this volume Nelson wryly recounts his initial disbelief upon being told that Herman Miller switched to modern because Rohde convinced management that "imitation of traditional designs was insincere aesthetically." In 1944, when Gilbert Rohde died, Herman Miller was making modern furniture exclusively. Casting around for a new designer, De Pree was impressed by an article on storage, published in *The Architectural Forum* and written by its two managing editors, Henry Wright and George Nelson. He got in touch with Nelson and, impressed by the quality of his thinking, hired him as Herman Miller's consultant design director. Nelson, trained as an architect and employed as an editor, had designed almost nothing and knew little about furniture. He prepared for the job by using his editorial position to research and write a survey on the furniture industry in America.

As design director, Nelson almost immediately began introducing new design concepts to the company. He also introduced other designers with new concepts of their own to fill out the line. The 1948 collection included some three pieces by the Hungarian architect Paul László, which had been designed to fit spaces he had designed. The team of Peter Hvidt and O.M. Nielsen are represented in this collection with laminated wood pieces manufactured by Fritz Hansen in Denmark. The sculptor Isamu Noguchi has work in both collections. But the bulk of the collection was designed by the Nelson office and by Charles and Ray Eames, whom Nelson had brought to Herman Miller in 1946.

That year The Museum of Modern Art had mounted a ground breaking show of Eames's furniture, and three years later Charles and Ray designed the first of The Museum of Modern Art's "Good Design" exhibitions directed by the critic Edgar Kauffmann Jr. For Herman Miller they set the tone of elegant surprise that dominates this catalog, but they also accomplished something far more important. The Eameses' served as a small, independent research laboratory whose prodding prepared the company and the furniture industry for the later research that led to the systems furniture that Herman Miller chiefly makes now. Had it not been for the inquiring zest of Nelson and Eames, it is unlikely that even Herman Miller would have retained, in 1960, the inventor Robert Propst to set up the furniture industry's first research corporation. That operation resulted in the systems furniture that, in the following decade, transformed the company and the office furniture industry.

Other manufacturers—notably Knoll with designs by Eero Saarinen and Dunbar with designs by Edward Wormley—were pioneering modern furniture brilliantly. Herman Miller did not stand out by its willingness to embrace new forms but by design approach informed less by dogma than by curiosity. Nelson asked, What if you put a typewriter on a surface that was an adjunct to a desk? What if you made a record player that was compatible with other things in the room, neither hidden nor dramatized? Eames asked, Can you mold compound curves in plywood? The sculptor Isamu Noguchi, with the interpretive grace he brought to his art, asked, If a coffee table has a beautiful sculptural base, why not give it a glass top so you can see the base?

These were design questions, not catalog questions; but they became the latter because the catalog had to be multifunctional. Directed to customers, retailers, and designer-specifiers, Herman Miller had to face up to the absence of a trained, broadly distributed group of people who knew how to specify and sell modern furniture. Like Knoll, Heywood Wakefield, and Dunbar, Herman Miller had made an audacious commitment to a style of furniture for which there was no demonstrable acceptance at the time. Since no audience existed, one had to be invented, or at least prepared. The consequences went beyond the residential furniture produced between the wars to include the office furniture of the future. Any truly different product requires that customers learn how to use it and that merchants learn how to sell it. Today, architectural and interior design offices have librarians in charge of catalogs and other specification materials. Corporations today have facility managers. But this catalog had the burden of explaining a concept that was new to most people and to many designers. It turned out to be, by default, an extremely useful design text, outlining a philosophy that design schools were just discovering. "Problem solving" was a fresh perspective before it became the cliché it is today. One of the lessons inherent in the catalog is that design is not fluff, not decoration, but a process for producing useful goods. Because, as Eames pointed out, the aesthetic is significantly useful, design was genuinely concerned with style. But it was far less concerned with styling. So the best modern furniture came to have the inevitability characteristic of Shaker furniture, both derived more from a particular view of life than from a proclivity towards a particular style. Mass produced furniture rarely has the overwhelming clarity and purity of Shaker furniture. But, since Shaker furniture, like the Shakers themselves, was produced in small runs, there is not much of it, nor many of them, around. Some of the objects shown here probably come as close as anyone reasonably could to incorporating craft ideals into the mass production of everyday things for everyday life.

Those are all reasons enough to celebrate the resurrection of this volume. But it is significant in another way as well. I doubt that anyone at Herman Miller noticed it at the time, and I have no reason to believe that he did either, but with this catalog George Nelson had written his first book.

Ralph Caplan

the herman miller collection 1952

the herman **M** iller

furniture designed by George Nelson and Charles Eames, with occasional pieces by Isamu Noguchi, Peter Hvidt and O. M. Nielsen

collection

the herman miller furniture co., Zeeland, Michigan

showrooms One Park Avenue, New York; 622 Merchandise Mart, Chicago

Exhibitors' Building, Grand Rapids; 8806 Beverly Boulevard, Los Angeles

sales offices 4300 Cedarwood Road, Minneapolis, Minn.; 819 Drexel Ave., San Antonio, Texas

2401 West 86th Terrace, Kansas City, Missouri; 19 Baltimore Place, Northwest, Atlanta, Georgia

1265 Fernandez Juncos Ave., Santurce, Puerto Rico

Copyright 1952 by Herman Miller Furniture Co., Zeeland, Michigan

foreword

From the viewpoint of the designer, which is the only viewpoint I can assume with any degree of propriety, the Herman Miller Furniture Company is a rather remarkable institution. Seen solely as a business enterprise, it is probably indistinguishable from thousands of others scattered through the U.S. It is a small company, it is located in a small town, its production facilities are adequate but not unusual, and it is run by the people who own it. What *is* remarkable about this enterprise is its philosophy — an attitude so deeply felt that to the best of my knowledge it has never been formulated.

Stated in its bare essentials, this philosophy — like others that have been solidly based — is so simple that it sounds almost naive. But it is not widely held by business, and perhaps it would be naive if it were not so astonishingly effective. This company today occupies a very solid position as a manufacturer of modern furniture and enjoys a prestige all out of proportion to its size. The attitude that governs Herman Miller's behavior, as far as I can make out, is compounded of the following set of principles:

What you make is important. Herman Miller, like all other companies, is governed by the rules of the American economy, but I have yet to see quality of construction or finish skimped to meet a popular price bracket, or for any other reason. Also, while the company has materially expanded its production, the limits of this expansion will be set by the size of the market that will accept Herman Miller's kind of furniture — the product will not be changed to expand the business.

Design is an integral part of the business. In this company's scheme of things, the designer's decisions are as important as those of the sales or production departments. If the design is changed, it is with the designer's participation and approval. There is no pressure on him to modify design to meet the market.

The product must be honest. Herman Miller discontinued production of period reproductions almost twelve years ago because its designer, Gilbert Rohde, had convinced the management that imitation of traditional designs was insincere aesthetically. (I couldn't believe this story when I first heard it, but after my experience of the past few years, I know it is true.)

You decide what you will make. Herman Miller has never done any consumer research or any pre-testing of its products to determine what the market "will accept." If designer and management like a solution to a particular furniture problem, it is put into production. There is no attempt to conform to the so-called norms of "public taste," nor any special faith in the methods used to evaluate the "buying public." The reason many people are struck by the freshness of Herman Miller designs is that the company is not playing follow-the-leader. Its designers are therefore not hamstrung by management's fear of getting out of step. All that is asked of the designer is a valid solution.

There is a market for good design. This assumption has been more than confirmed, but it took a great deal of courage to make it and stick to it. The fact is that in furniture as in many other fields, there is a substantial segment of the public that is well in advance of the manufacturers. But few producers dare to believe it.

In this outline of an attitude, you will no doubt recognize several familiar patterns: there is a hint of the craftsman as opposed to the industrialist; there is a suggestion of the "better mousetrap" theory in another form, and the rugged individual with convictions is in evidence throughout. But if the philosophy sounds somewhat archaic, it is interesting to see its manifestations in terms of the furniture shown in this book. It is unlikely that any person would be equally enthusiastic — or unenthusiastic — about every piece shown, but I think it would be difficult not to conclude that the company had a real interest in exploiting some of the possibilities open to furniture today in the areas of design, materials and techniques. The furniture shown here is the result of a *program* as well as a philosophy. The program includes an assumption that plywood and lumber are only two of a whole range of materials suitable for furniture. A considerable amount of experimental design work is being done on new pieces that explore the possibilities of others. It also assumes that the program is strengthened by the participation of a group of designers who share Herman Miller's particular attitudes. I believe that the range of the collection — from Noguchi's sculptured table to Hvidt and Neilsen's impeccably crafted pieces to Eames' magnificent designs in molded wood, metal, and plastic—could never be encompassed by a single designer, for the various underlying approaches, while related, are too intensely personal. A final word on the Herman Miller program: its goal is a *permanent* collection designed to meet fully the requirements for modern living. The collection is to be permanent in the sense that it will not be scrapped for each market, or for each new "trend" as announced by the style experts. It is designed to grow, not necessarily in size, but in the perfection of its component parts. No piece will be kept if a better design can be developed to take its place, nor will a given way of making things be followed simply because that's the way they were always made. Also, ways of living are continually changing. Again, I think, the material in this book suggests the attitude more clearly than any statement.

There is one other point that may be of interest to those concerned with problems of design: by far the largest part of the collection was designed by people trained in architecture. It may be no more than coincidence, and I must certainly confess to prejudice in this regard, but there is this to be said for the architectural approach to any design problem, and particularly that of furniture: the problem is never seen in isolation. The design process is always related on the one hand to the houses or other structures in which the furniture is to be used, and on the other to the people who will use it. When successfully followed through, the approach of the architect-in-industry goes much deeper than styling and is far more likely to create trends than to follow them. To reinforce this point it is not necessary to use only the Herman Miller program as an example. The work of Alvar Aalto, Marcel Breuer, Eero Saarinen and many others could be cited.

A word about this book. It is primarily an illustrated record of furniture currently in production, and as such it has been planned for convenient use by those whose business it is to purchase or specify furniture. It is also intended as a guide for professionals such as architects and interior designers. In addition to photographic illustrations, the book presents full dimensional data, so that the relationship of rooms and furniture can be accurately studied. Design students, it is hoped, will find the book equally valuable as a reference.

All material for the book was assembled and prepared by various members of the Herman Miller Furniture Company. In planning the layout and typography of the book, I found that the restraint exercised in the choice and amount of written material most unusual in a manufacturer given an opportunity to talk about his product. Here as elsewhere the Herman Miller philosophy is manifest: let the furniture speak for itself.

George Nelson

preface to the second edition

As this second edition of "The Herman Miller Collection" goes to press, it is a little hard to remember the way things were four years ago, when this book was first being prepared. A very small furniture manufacturer, who had been quietly doing a rather extraordinary pioneering job, had introduced a complete new collection of modern furniture in January of 1947 and was suddenly caught up in a kind of publicity the company had never enjoyed and a volume of demand which had never been anticipated. It would be agreeable if Herman Miller's design group could take to itself the credit for this swift success, but other factors were also in operation. During the latter years of the war the population of the country had developed an unprecedented power to buy, and even more important in this instance, the long, slow development of public taste began to accelerate in a remarkable way. Herman Miller, as one of a tiny handful of companies which had been building modern furniture with conviction and understanding, inevitably found itself the focus of a kind of attention all out of proportion to its size.

With this attention came demands. For instance, innumerable requests for detailed information on the furniture in the collection. It looks a little strange as I write this, but at the time we had no information. Come to think of it, we didn't have much except furniture — and there was precious little of that after the first month. There was no advertising manager, no active advertising agency, no budget for promotion . . . it was an interesting situation. We were flaunting all the rules of U.S. business, and business was terrific. Fortunately no one made the mistake of assuming that business was terrific *because* we were flaunting the rules.

To meet the problem of providing information, my office switched overnight from the design of furniture to the design of a book about furniture. It might be asked why a group of architects-turned-furniture designers complicated their existence further by taking a fling at graphic design. The main reason is that I had talked to a few advertising agencies with topflight art directors and when they heard the size of the Herman Miller account I was politely evicted. So we had to do the job — at that time there was no one else. In a way we were not so badly off, for we had a very strong conviction that the design of the book had to reflect the character of the furniture. Even at the beginning we were sure that the Herman Miller program had to be all of a piece. Today we are still sure of it.

After a while the book got designed and we felt pretty good about it. There were some seventy pages of handsome photographs and we put them in stiff covers and a dust jacket. Cost was a factor which had been shoved aside in the excitement, and when the printers finally told us, we had a figure price which bore no possible relationship to any budget the company might afford. So we put a price on the book. Had we been more experienced in these matters, I imagine we would never have dared, for such a practice was unheard of. But we did, and as one printing after another was exhausted we began to realize that people understood what we were doing and why. A good thing about having convictions is that one tends to act on them.

Now some time has passed, and there is a new book. It is quite a bit larger than the original edition. There is much new furniture in the household group. Furniture for offices — the Executive Office Group — has become an important addition to the collection. The BSC system, an arrangement for using Herman Miller's basic storage components in storage walls, provides the beginning of a transition from portable to built-in furniture. A newcomer to the collection is the Hansen group from Denmark. Designed by Hvidt-Neilsen, these laminated wood pieces fall into the best Scandinavian tradition and are magnificently constructed. Herman Miller considers itself a producer rather than a distributor, but it seemed desirable to make an exception in the case of a European manufacturer whose attitudes on design and manufacturing conform so closely to its own.

The original Eames group whose nucleus was the famous molded wood and metal chair has expanded tremendously. There are the Eames storage units, the new plastic chair and, most recently introduced, the chairs in welded wire. These and other new designs are giving the entire collection a greater range and flexibility than it has ever had before.

George Nelson

George Nelson was trained as an architect and found himself in the field of furniture design as the result of a series of accidents, most of which appear to have been caused by an acute dislike for specialized activity. Educated at Yale, he won the Rome Prize in architecture in 1932 while doing postgraduate work at Catholic University. The following two years were spent in Europe and devoted largely to travel, the study of Italian, and sketching antique monuments. The last of these activities resulted in so great an admiration for the architecture of the past that he became a convinced modernist, as he felt that there was no point whatever in trying to beat the ancients at their own game. One outcome of the stay abroad was a series of twelve articles based on interviews with the outstanding modern architects of Europe. Published on his return, the articles attracted the attention of the publisher of The Architectural Forum, and he presently joined the staff. While no longer with the magazine, Nelson still retains the position of consultant to the Forum.

An architectural office was opened in 1936, in association with William Hamby, and a number of commissions, chiefly residential, were executed. Some of this work has been exhibited and published as far afield as Cairo, Moscow and Stockholm. With the outbreak of the war the architectural work had to be put aside and the next few years were taken up with a variety of activities — editorial work, a book (Tomorrow's House, written in collaboration with Henry Wright) and design commissions for industrial concerns. As a by-product of the book, the Storagewall was developed and presented by Life magazine. Basically the Storagewall was a replacement of the conventional partition by a series of storage units which functioned as both wall and containers for all sorts of household items. It was publication of this design that led to the association with the Herman Miller Furniture Company. Nelson worked through most of 1945 and all of 1946 developing a large collection of furniture, and found the time in between to produce an article on the furniture industry which was published by Fortune. The article was received by the industry with feelings that might best be described as mixed. At the end of 1947 Nelson gave up his editorial work and opened up an office in New York for the practice of architecture and industrial design, thus giving full play to his disinclination to specialize.

The Nelson office is currently engaged in the design of showrooms, office interiors, houses, a variety of products, graphic arts (this book is a recent example) and is doing research in lightweight demountable structures. The furniture for Herman Miller was designed to be "a simple, direct expression of construction with existing techniques." Pieces now under development represent a departure from current practice in both construction and design.

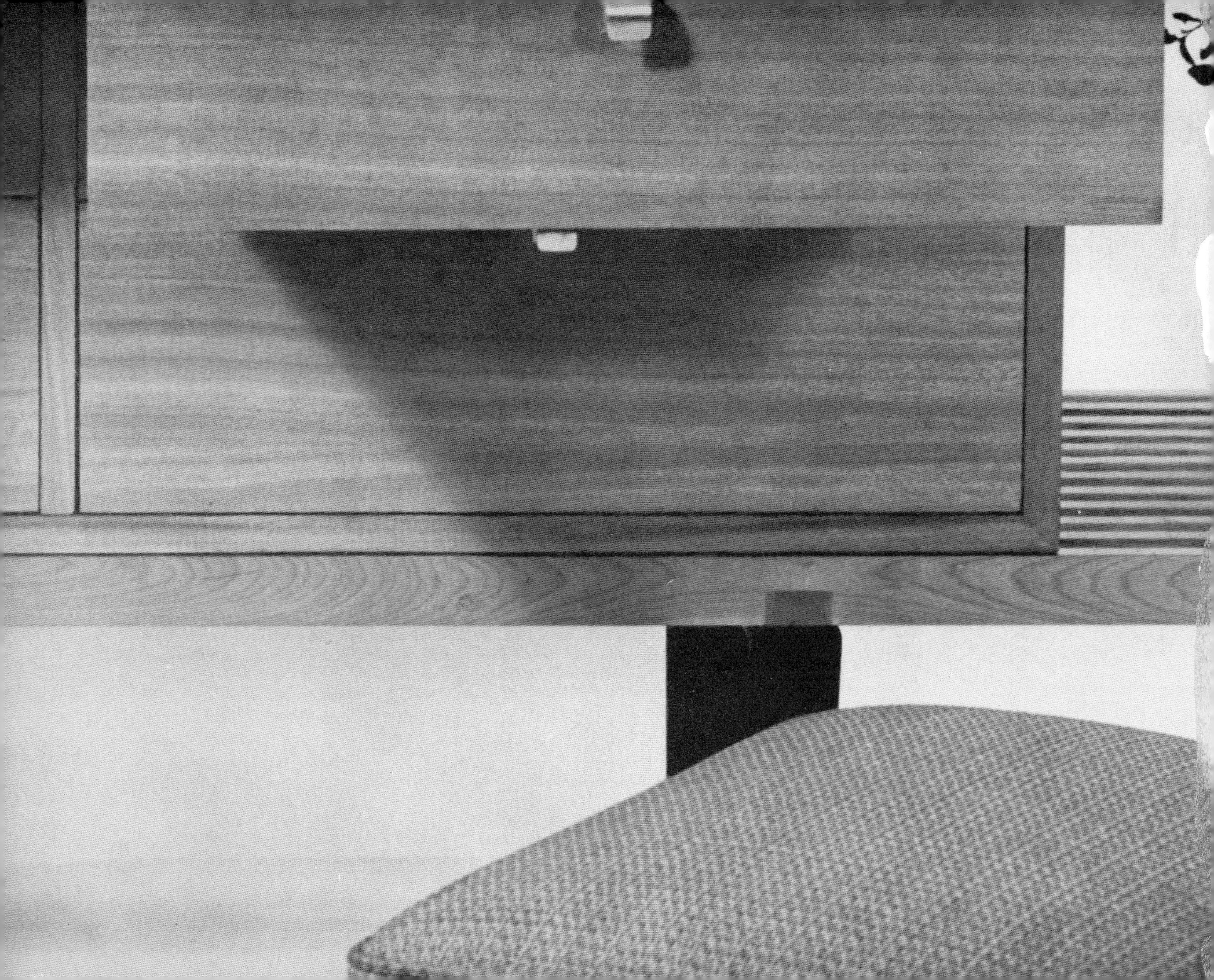

storage 1

The problem of what to put where is one that has constantly grown in importance in the design of interiors. Smaller homes and apartments, the developing taste for less cluttered rooms and the general increase in the number of possessions are three of the main factors which have contributed to the design of new storage furniture. The portable units illustrated in this section are intended primarily for already-built dwellings, and they have been so designed that a great many combinations of height and width can be obtained. These modular chests and cabinets, used on their own low bases or on the platform bench (left) can, if properly handled, increase the functional utility of any interior and at the same time greatly enhance its architectural background.

MODULAR CASE SIZES *(18½" deep)*

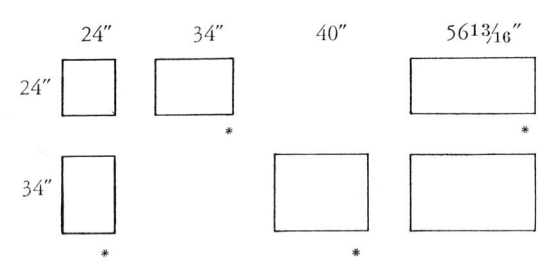

24"   34"   40"   56 13/16"

24" [ ] [   ]   [   ]
          *   *

34" [ ]   [   ]   [   ]
     *   *

also available 12" deep

OVERALL HEIGHTS *(case plus base)*

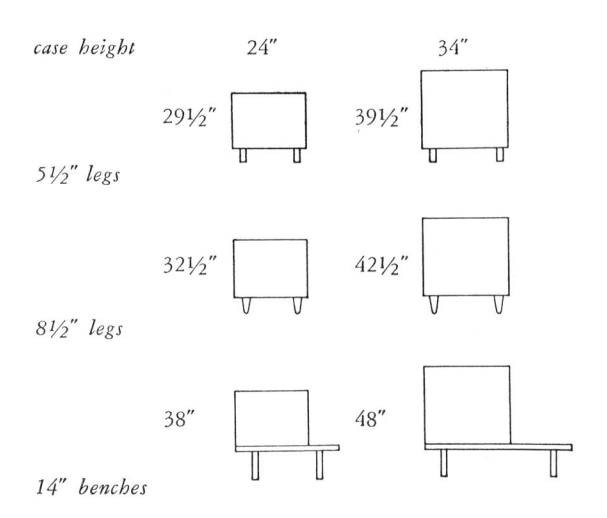

case height   24"   34"

5½" legs   29½"   39½"

8½" legs   32½"   42½"

14" benches   38"   48"

THE MODULAR SYSTEM (top, left) serves as a key to the Herman Miller case line. Diagrams on pp. 15-19 show the different groups in detail.

STANDARD WOOD FINISHES for shells and fronts of cases, and any other units as listed in individual specifications.
    Tawny Walnut (TW)   Comb Grain Oak (CGO)
    Chili Walnut (CW)   Ebonized (E)

STANDARD LACQUER COLORS for fronts of cases (the only finish on masonite sliding doors):
    Bittersweet Red (BR)   Forest Green (FG)   Gunmetal (GM)

FINISHES ON HARDWOOD for legs and frames of occasional tables and seating pieces:
    Tawny Walnut color (TWB)   Natural, to match CGO (B)
    Chili Walnut color (CWB)   Ebonized (E)

HARD PLASTIC TOPS: light grey, buff, mustard, turquoise and white

SPECIAL FINISHES are available at an additional charge of 15% (on our standard walnut and comb grain oak veneers only). A large sample of the desired finish should be submitted to Herman Miller Furniture Company for approval. Solid lacquer colors can also be matched.

FINISHED BACKS may be ordered for any of the cases at an additional charge (see price list).

REMOVABLE DRAWER DIVIDERS are furnished as follows:
    4610: center divider in top and third drawers
    4600, 4714, 4715: 3-section divider in top drawer
    4606, 4712, 4713: 6-section divider in top drawer and 3-section divider in bottom drawer
    4606-V: 3-section divider in bottom drawer
    4620, 4935, 4936: 6-section divider in top drawer and 3-section divider in third drawer.

BASES: Unless otherwise noted in diagrams on pp. 15-19, all cases may be set on platform benches (see p. 12) or the standard legs listed below. Diagram (bottom, left) shows overall heights of cases combined with the bases selected.
    512—5½" metal leg for 12" deep cases   818—8½" metal leg for 18½" deep cases
    518—5½" metal leg for 18½" deep cases   L-12—5½" wood leg for 12" deep cases
    812—8½" metal leg for 12" deep cases   L-18—5½" wood leg for 18½" deep cases
Metal legs are satin aluminum; wood legs are ebonized, unless otherwise specified.

HARDWARE: The pulls illustrated below and on facing page are chrome-plated. Nos. 1, 2 and 3 form a related group, as do Nos. 4 and 5. (Do not use No. 5 except on large doors.) No. 6 is a wood knob with a chrome-plated insert; the finish always matches the front to which the pull is applied. No. 1 pull is standard for all desk and radio-phonograph drop-lids.

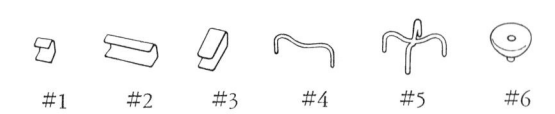

#1   #2   #3   #4   #5   #6

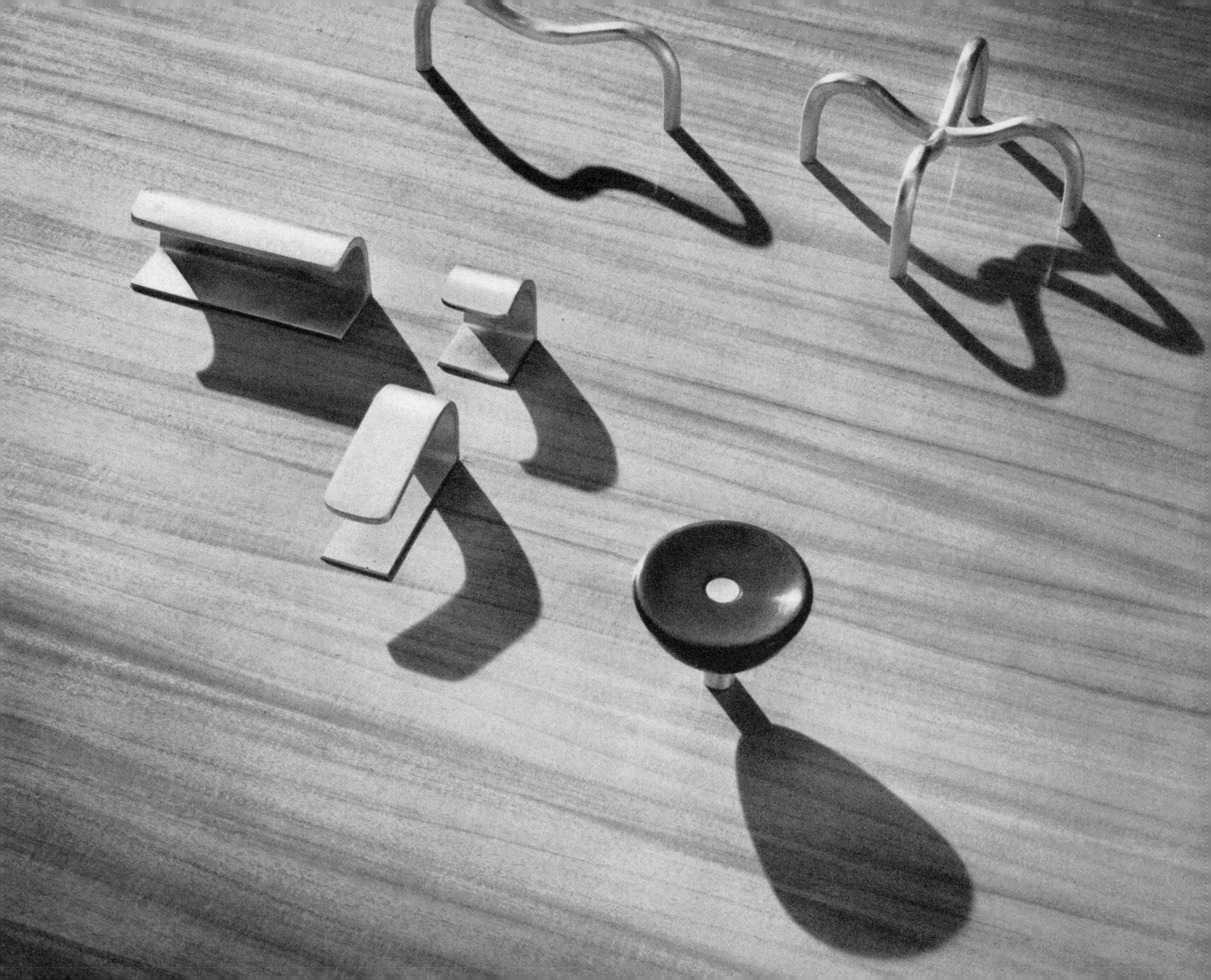

as a coffee table

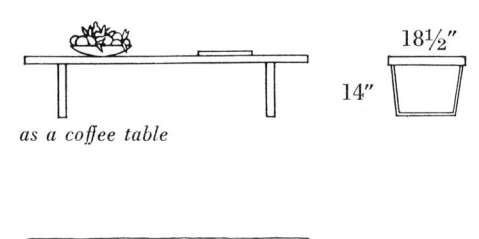

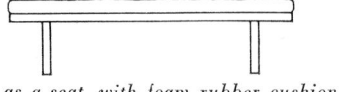

18½"
14"

as a seat, with foam rubber cushions

as a platform for storage units

The platform bench, shown here, is primarily a high base for deep and shallow cases, but it also serves as a low table and for extra seating. When used for seating it can be fitted with upholstered foam rubber cushions which are available in 24", 48" and 72" lengths (C-24, C-48, C-72). Natural finish on hardwood with ebonized legs (B) or all ebonized (E).

4690 — 48"	4692 — 72"
4991 — 56-3/16"	4992 — 92"
4691 — 68"	4693 — 102"

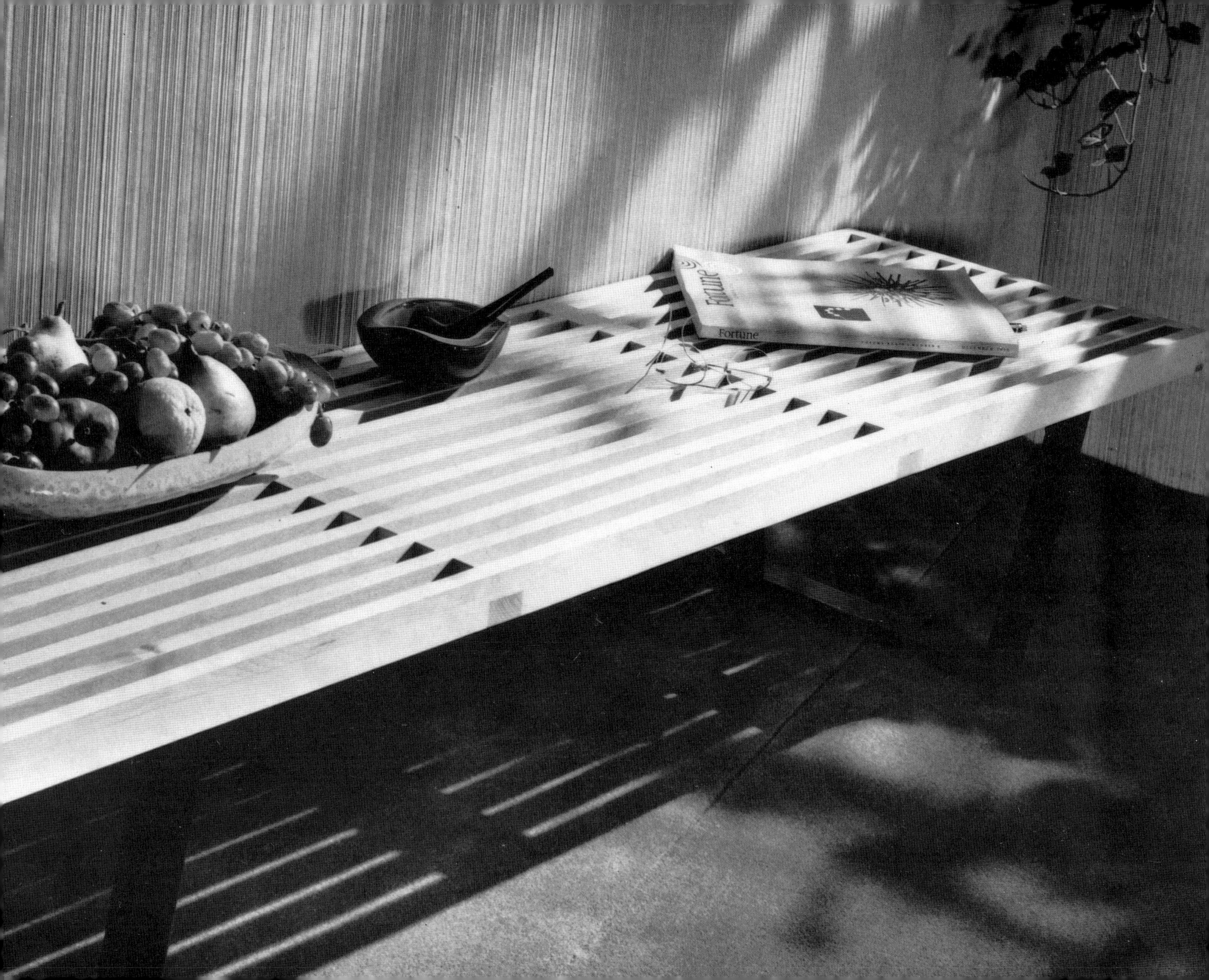
Fortune
Fortune

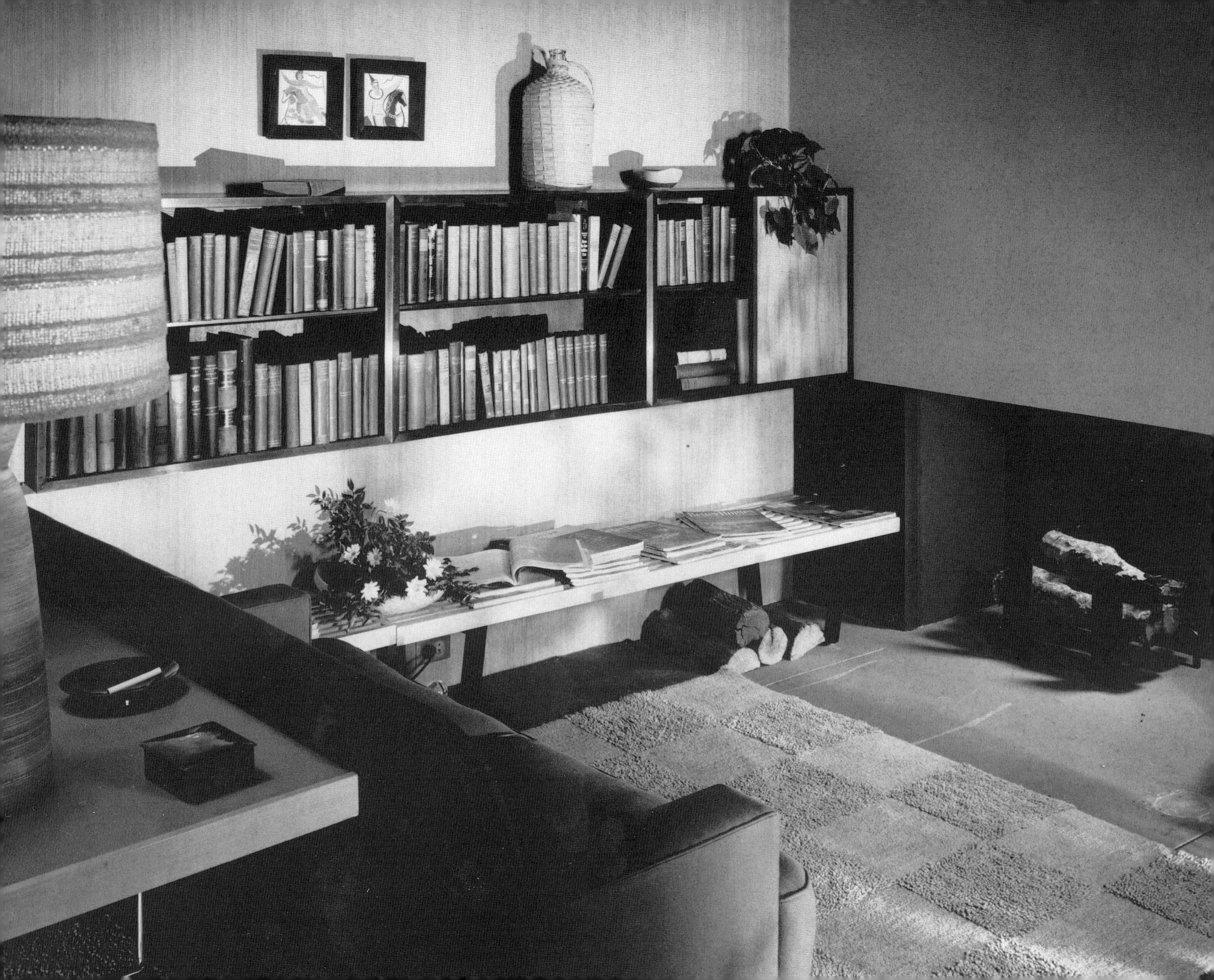

CASES *24" high, 12" deep*

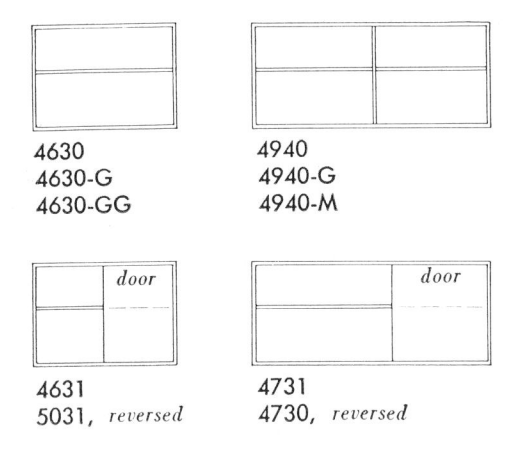

4630
4630-G
4630-GG

4940
4940-G
4940-M

4631
5031, *reversed*

4731
4730, *reversed*

CASES *34" high, 12" deep*

4635

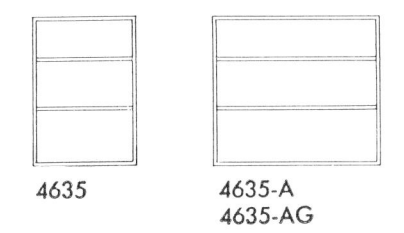

4635-A
4635-AG

The 12" deep units may be used on 5½" legs, 8½" legs or 14" high platform benches (right). If ordered for wall-hanging (facing p.) they will be furnished with a special cleat below top for fastening to wall. An additional cleat, cut to length of entire wall-hung assembly and painted to match wall color, should be supplied by purchaser and fastened to wall below cases to carry the load. Wall-hanging is not recommended for the 34" high bookcases or any of the 18½" deep storage units. Suffix "G": sliding glass doors. Suffix "GG": stationary glass back with sliding glass doors in front (for use as room divider). Suffix "M": masonite sliding doors in any of the standard lacquer finishes.

CASES 24" high
18½" deep

door

4702 (24")
specify door hinged left or right (facing)

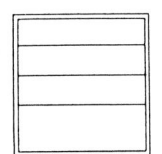

4701 (24")

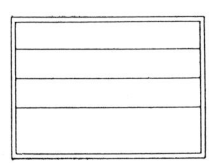

4606 (34")

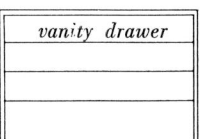

vanity drawer

4606-V (34")
(on 5½" legs only)

4606-V
4672 *bench*

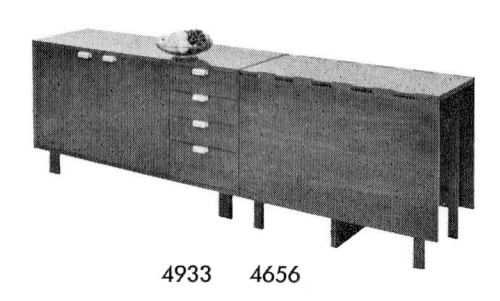

4933 4656

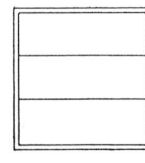

4700

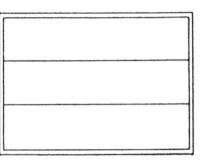

4600

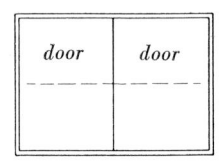

door	door

4601
5101 (open)

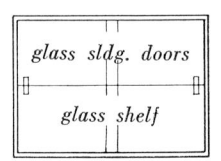

glass sldg. doors
glass shelf

4607-G
4607-GG *(with fixed glass back)*

4656 gateleg table lines up with the 24" cases on 5½" legs (see above); 18½" x 40" (closed), 29½" high. Fully extended it seats eight generously (40" x 64⅞") as illustrated on page 45.

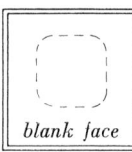

blank face

4702-TV

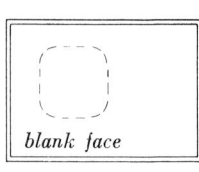

blank face

4601-TV

4691 *bench*   4710

4601-TV   4743

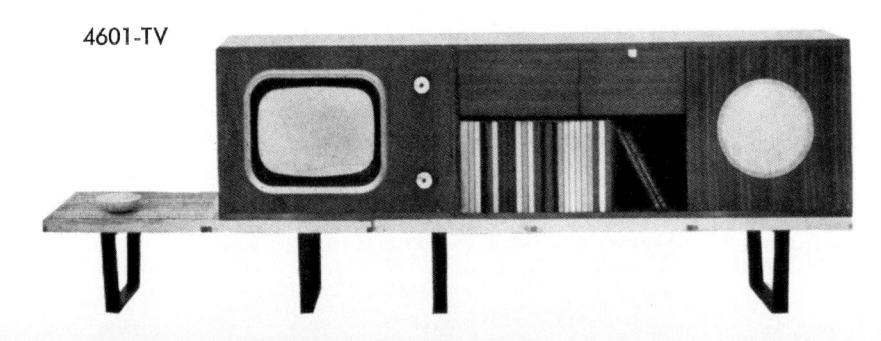

Cabinets for Television installation are equipped with blank face panels in which purchaser is to make necessary cut-outs and install his own equipment (speaker facing down); 8½" legs or platform benches.

16

4690 *bench*

4691 *bench*

Vanity drawer in 4606-V chest (facing page) runs on extension slides and contains fold-down mirror and cosmetic compartments (see also p. 38).

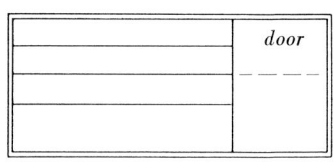

	door

4713 *(56-3/16")*
4712 *reversed*

Suspended vanity (right) for use with 24" high cases on 5½" legs only; fold-down mirror, fluorescent light and cosmetic compartments (p. 38).

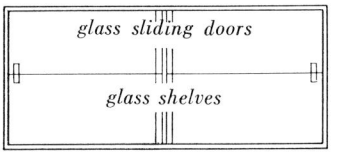

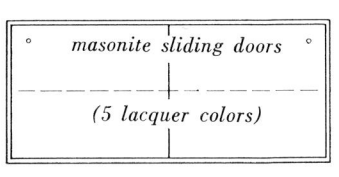

4702   4661   4698 *bench*   4700

glass sliding doors
glass shelves

4939-G

masonite sliding doors
(5 lacquer colors)

4939-M
4939 *(open)*

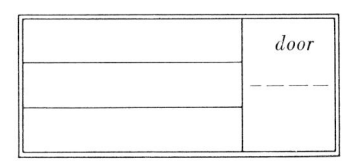

	door

4715
4714 *reversed*

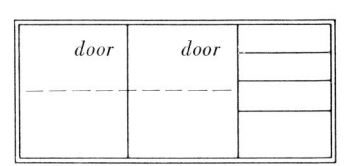

door	door	

4933
4934 *reversed*

door	books
	records

4710
4711 *reversed*

phono.	radio	
	records	

4743

Cabinet for phonograph-radio installation is equipped with blanks in which purchaser is to make necessary cut-outs and install his own equipment; cloth-covered opening for 15" speaker, 8½" legs or platform bench.

4992 *bench*   4743

pull-out desk	
	vanity dwr.

4901
(for use with platform bench only)

Guestroom unit, 24" x 57³⁄₁₆", 18½" deep; projecting platform bench provides convenient space for luggage.

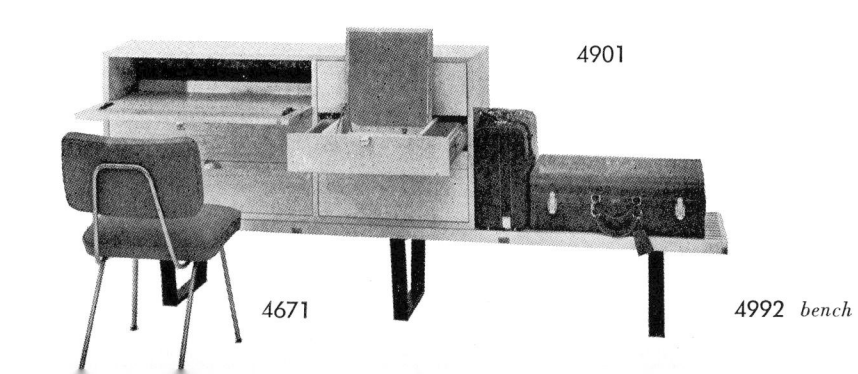

4901

4671   4992 *bench*

17

CASES *34" high*
18½" deep

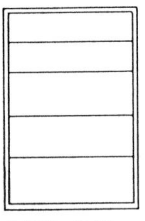

4610 (24")

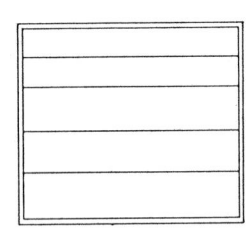

4620 (40")

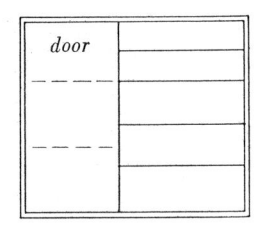

door

4622 (40")
4622-J *with hanger*
4621 *reversed*
4621-J " *with hgr.*

4625-A

4610

4621-J

door | door

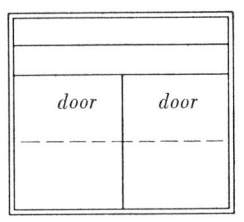

4626

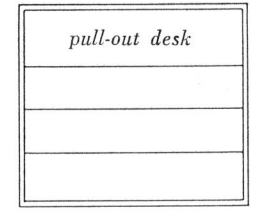

pull-out desk

4623
(on 5½" legs only)

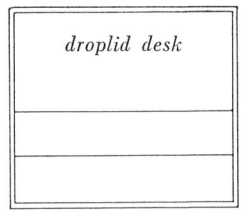

droplid desk

4624
4624-L *with desk light*
(on platform bench only)

Sliding hanger for children's clothes is provided in chest-cabinets 4621-J (above), 4622-J, 4935-J and 4936-J. Cabinet for Television installation (right) has blank face panel in which purchaser is to make necessary cut-outs and install his own equipment (speaker facing down); see also p. 69.

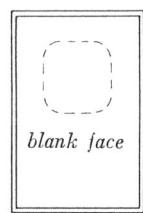

blank face

4613-TV

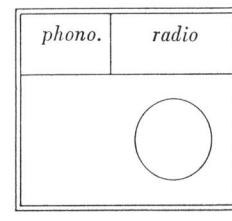

phono. | radio

4741

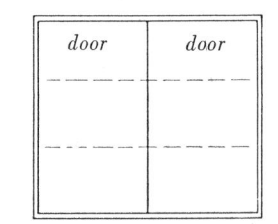

door | door

4625-A

door | door

two trays

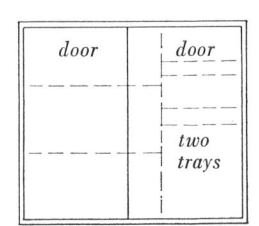

4625

4625

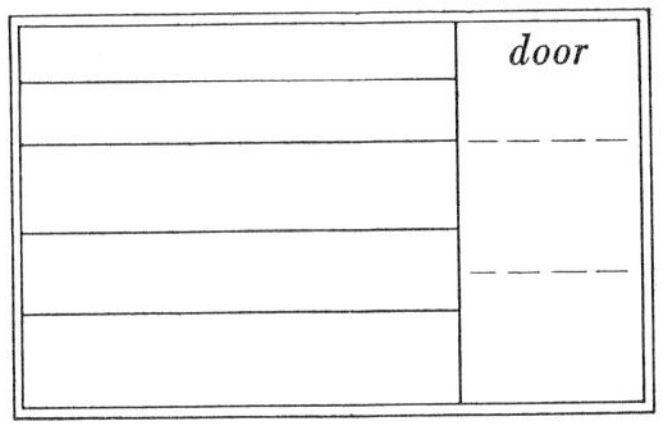

	door

4935 *(56-3/16")*
4935-J *with hanger*
4936 *reversed*
4936-J *" with hgr.*

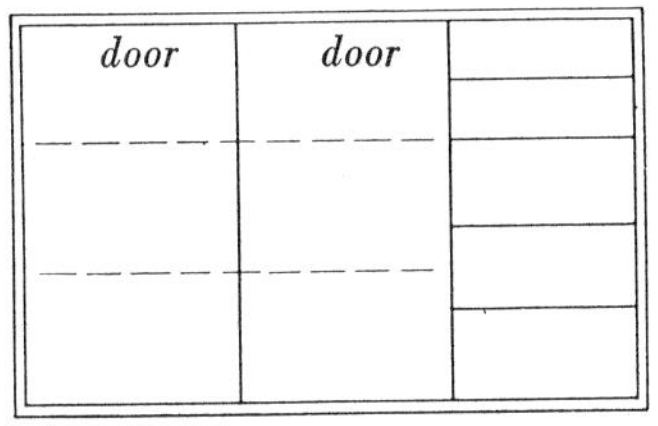

door	door	

4937-A *(56-3/16")*
4938-A *reversed*

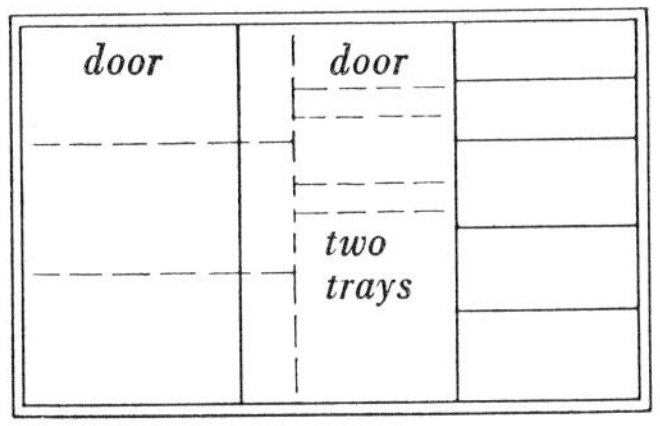

door	door	
	two trays	

4937 *(56-3/16")*
4938 *reversed*

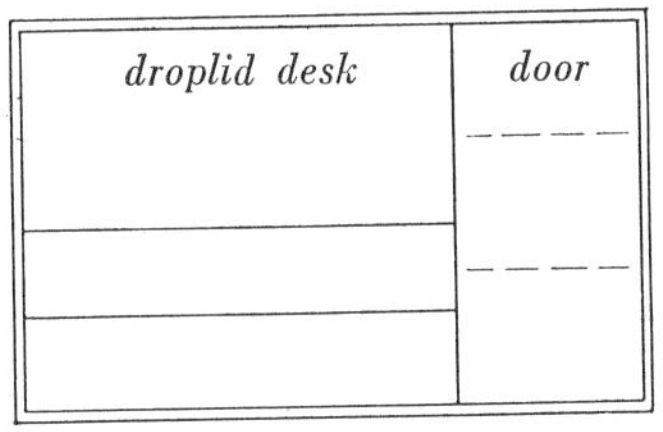

droplid desk	door

4931   4932 *reversed*
4931-L, 4932-L *with desk light*
(on platform bench only)

Chest desks are furnished with ebonized pigeonhole units. Built-in fluorescent desk lights may be ordered for two models (see also pp. 72-73).

4691 *bench*   4610   4931   4690 *bench*   5069 *chair*

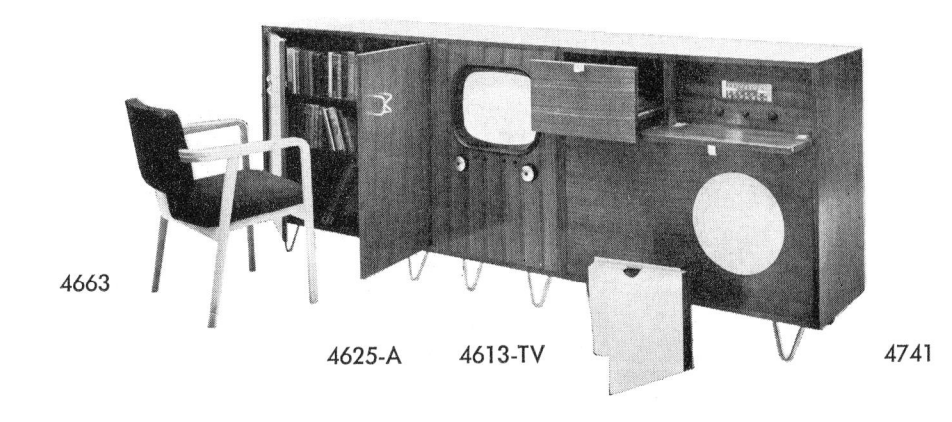

4663   4625-A   4613-TV   4741

Cabinet for phonograph-radio installation (left) is equipped with blanks in phonograph slide and radio face in which purchaser is to make necessary cut-outs and install his own equipment; cloth-covered opening for 15" speaker is provided. 4625-A may serve as matching cabinet for record storage.

19

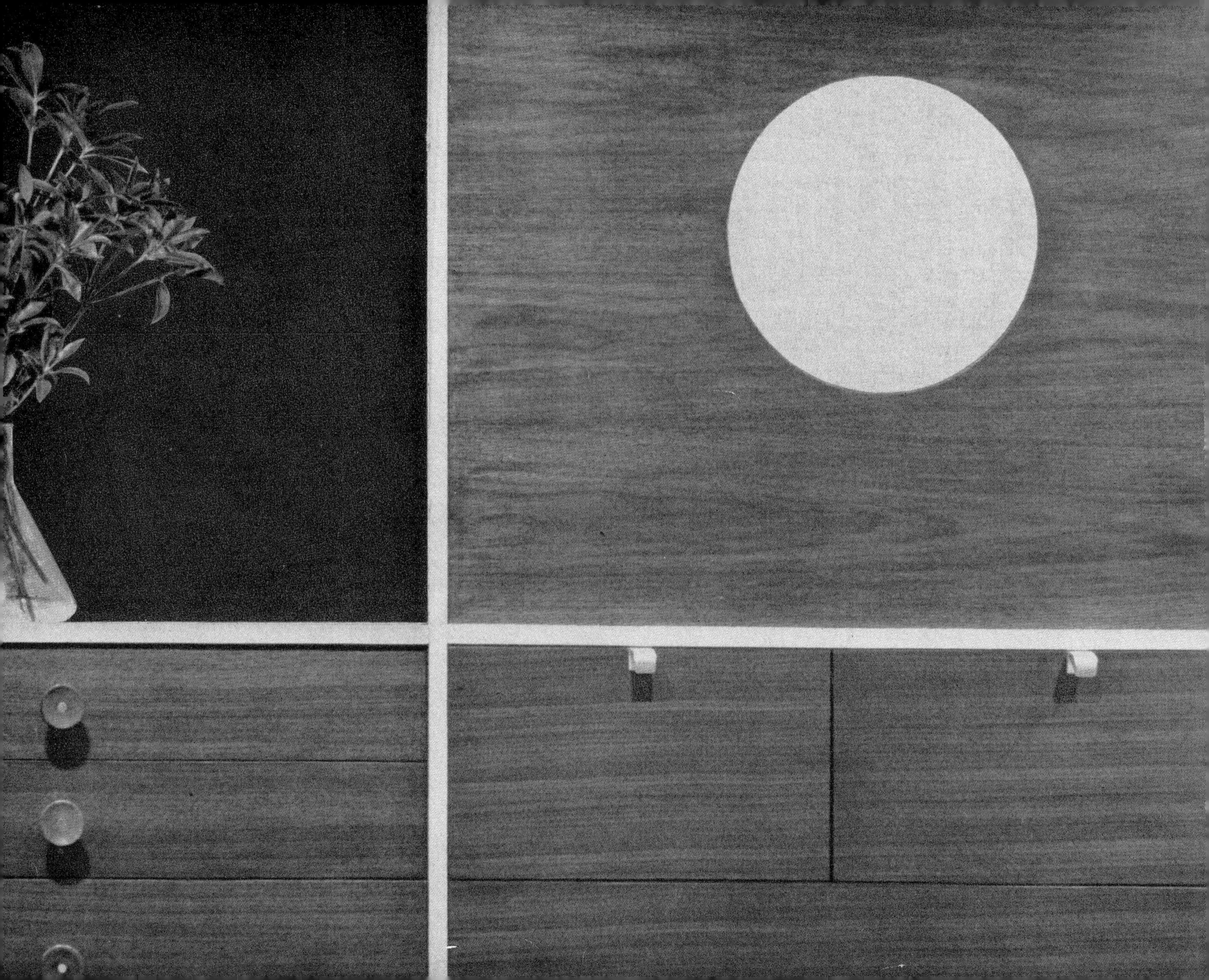

storage 2

The storage wall is a major addition to the tools at the disposal of the architect and designer. Replacing both room partitions and furniture, it can add literally hundreds of cubic feet of storage space to a dwelling without reducing the effective size of the rooms it serves. It can do this, moreover, at a lower unit cost than the furniture it replaces. In modern residential work, consequently, use of this element is rapidly increasing. The components made available in the Herman Miller Collection are identical in design, finish and quality with those in the furniture, thus guaranteeing both designer and owner not only satisfactory long-term performance but unexcelled appearance as well. In the following pages the components available are listed, along with illustrations of a number of uses.

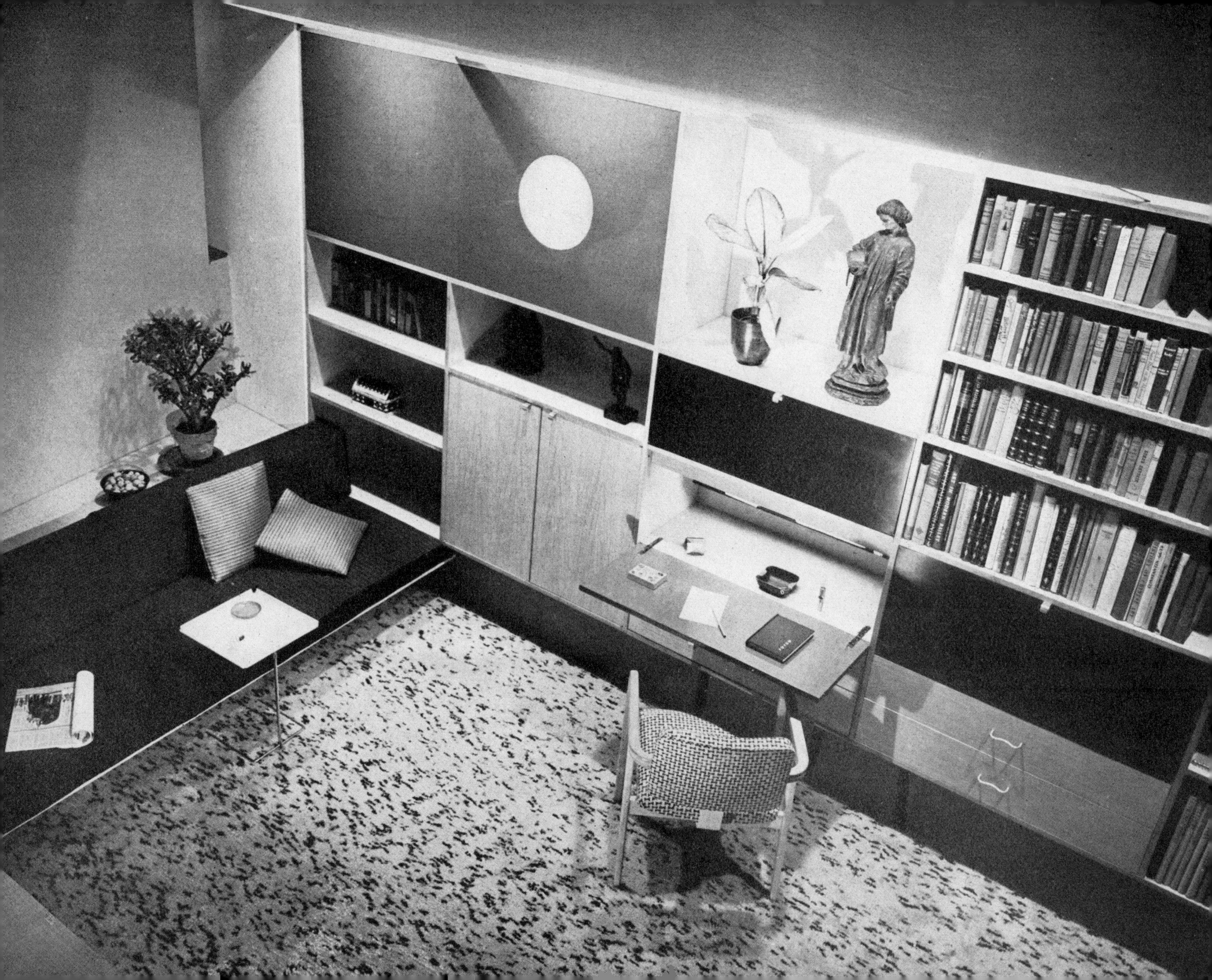

the herman miller system of basic storage components

BSC — Basic Storage Components — is the designation given a simple, yet remarkably flexible system for creating custom-designed and built storage walls at production prices. The elements in the BSC system include drawers, cabinet doors, drop-front desks, radio panels and a variety of accessories.

BSC components are identical in quality with the furniture which earned Herman Miller an international reputation. They were designed for use in interiors where the finest workmanship and finish is required. The room opposite, commissioned by Detroit's Art Institute, is a representative example.

The use of built-in storage is one of the most important developments in modern architecture and interior design. It releases space, is more economical than equivalent storage in portable furniture, reduces maintenance and housekeeping time, and, to the contemporary eye, is more satisfying esthetically. The purpose of BSC is to accept and further this trend by making available to the design professions mass-produced storage components of the highest quality at modest prices.

The following pages contain all necessary information for the design of storage walls and other built-in installations. The framework, a simple grid of plywood, is arranged to take the various required combinations of BSC components. The frame should be produced locally, by a mill or cabinet maker; in many instances it is built by the contractor on the job. Where special conditions or problems are encountered the experience of the Herman Miller Furniture Company is at the disposal of the architect or designer.

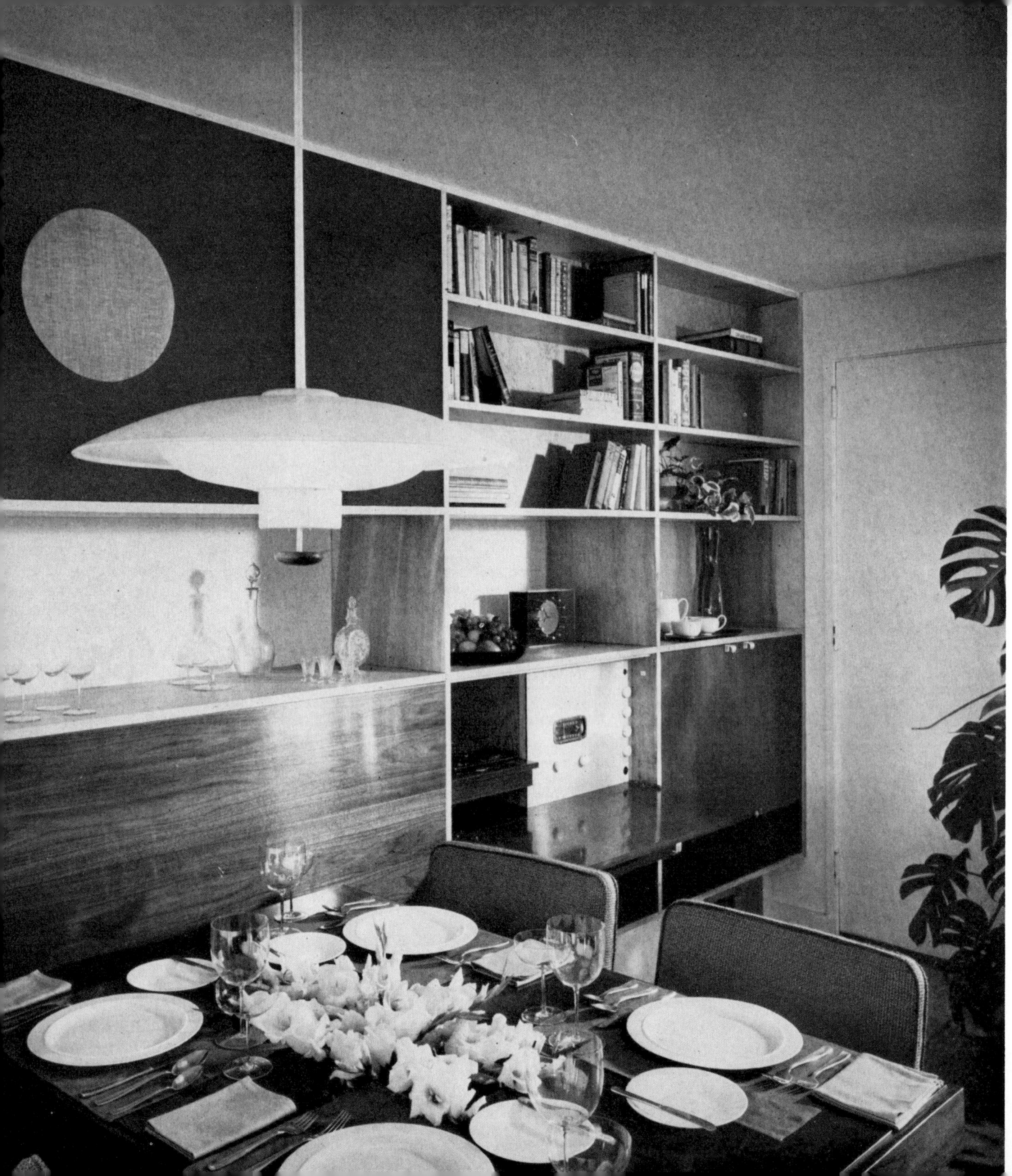

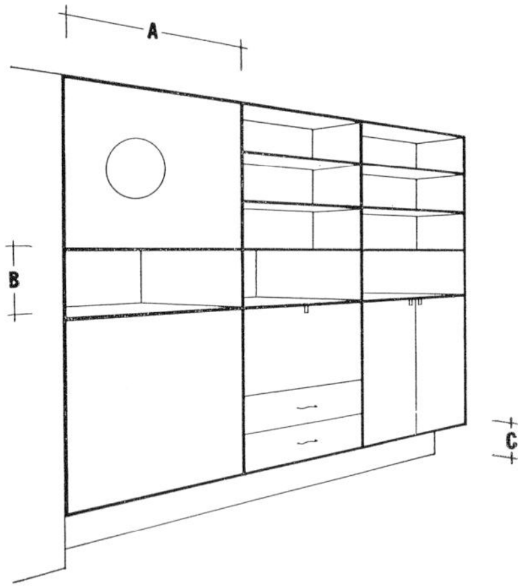
A
B
C

The installation shown is in a living-dining room and contains a radio, record-player, drawers, cabinets and open shelving. The diagram at left indicates some of the methods used to adjust a BSC storage wall to the space it has to fit. Vertical section "A" contains a speaker panel and, below, a blank panel: these may be ordered to size (see page 29) thus permitting adjustments in width. "B" is an open shelf section whose height can be varied without disturbing the standard components. The base "C" can be either 5" or 12½" in height (see pages 28 and 29).

Where built-in television is planned, the standard BSC depth of 18½" can be increased to accommodate the tube.

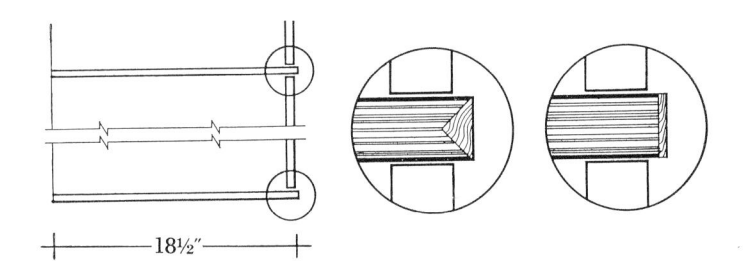

Best material for framework is 13/16" plywood. It may be edge-banded in either of the ways shown above. Minimum depth for frame is 18½" and all drawers and other inserts should be set back ¼". No special provision is needed for drawers. The wood slides furnished with the drawers attach directly to the sides of the frame, and also stop the drawers when closed. Typical installation procedure is shown at right. Place group of drawers on end to determine position of slides allowing for adequate clearances between drawer fronts. (Overall heights of arrangements shown on pages 28-29 include all necessary clearances between the individual components.) Transfer measurements to inside of frame and fasten slides.

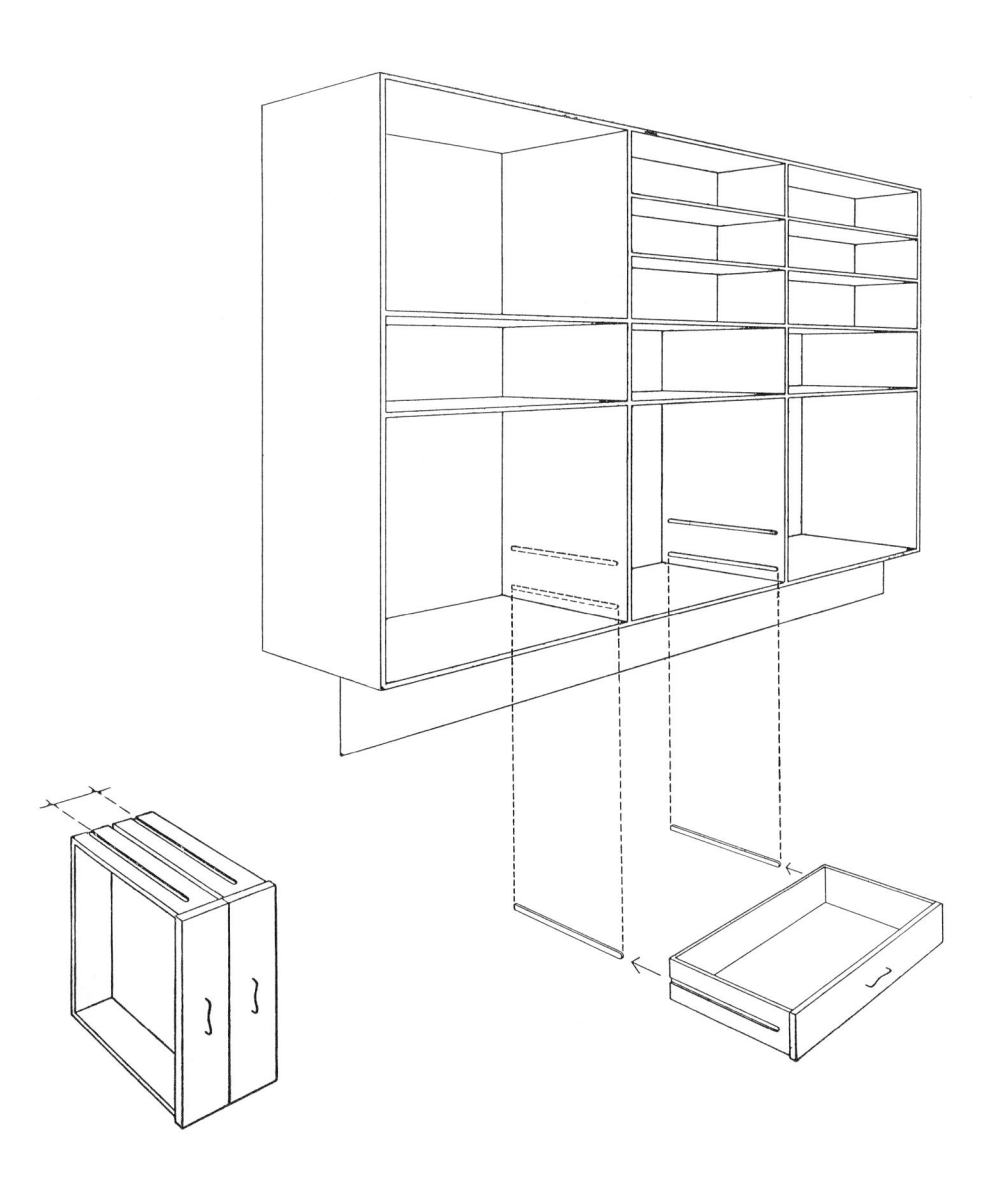

The drop front desk above is a particularly desirable feature where space in the room does not make it possible to use a free standing desk, or where a work space that can be put out of sight, is needed. Accessories include pigeonhole unit for stationery and fluorescent desk light.

In addition to the usual storage facilities provided in cabinets, drawers and open shelves, the BSC system permits the accommodation of sound and vision equipment, desks and vanity units.

Where radio and television are needed the BSC wall is particularly efficient, for it not only eliminates the bulky furniture generally supplied but allows the creation of sound chambers large enough to permit speakers to function properly. Few if any commercial sets contain sound chambers that are adequate in size. With BSC units it is possible to incorporate any desired amount of electronic equipment. In most cases the standard BSC minimum depth of 18½" is sufficient; for large television tubes this depth may have to be increased. Where a stud wall is located behind a BSC unit it is often possible to gain the needed extra depth by using the stud space.

One of the most useful applications of the BSC system, as shown on facing page, is a wall-to-wall window height arrangement containing drawer storage and a special suspended vanity (#4661). The vanity unit measures 18½" x 30" (top) and 5 13/16" (high), and contains a full size mirror, cosmetic compartments and a fluorescent lamp which turns on automatically when cover is lifted. To insure proper height for vanity, the adjoining drawer units should be on a 5½" base.

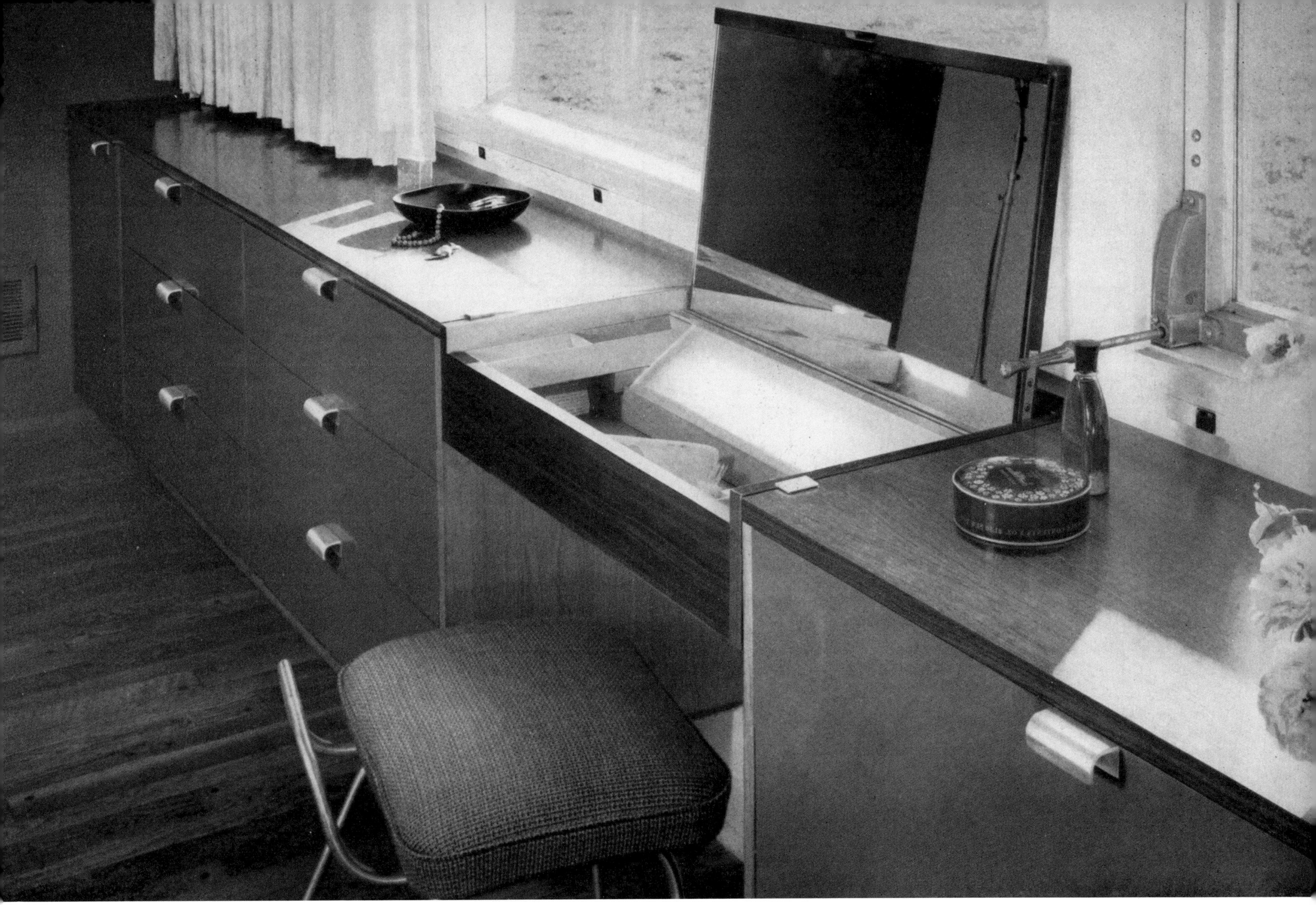

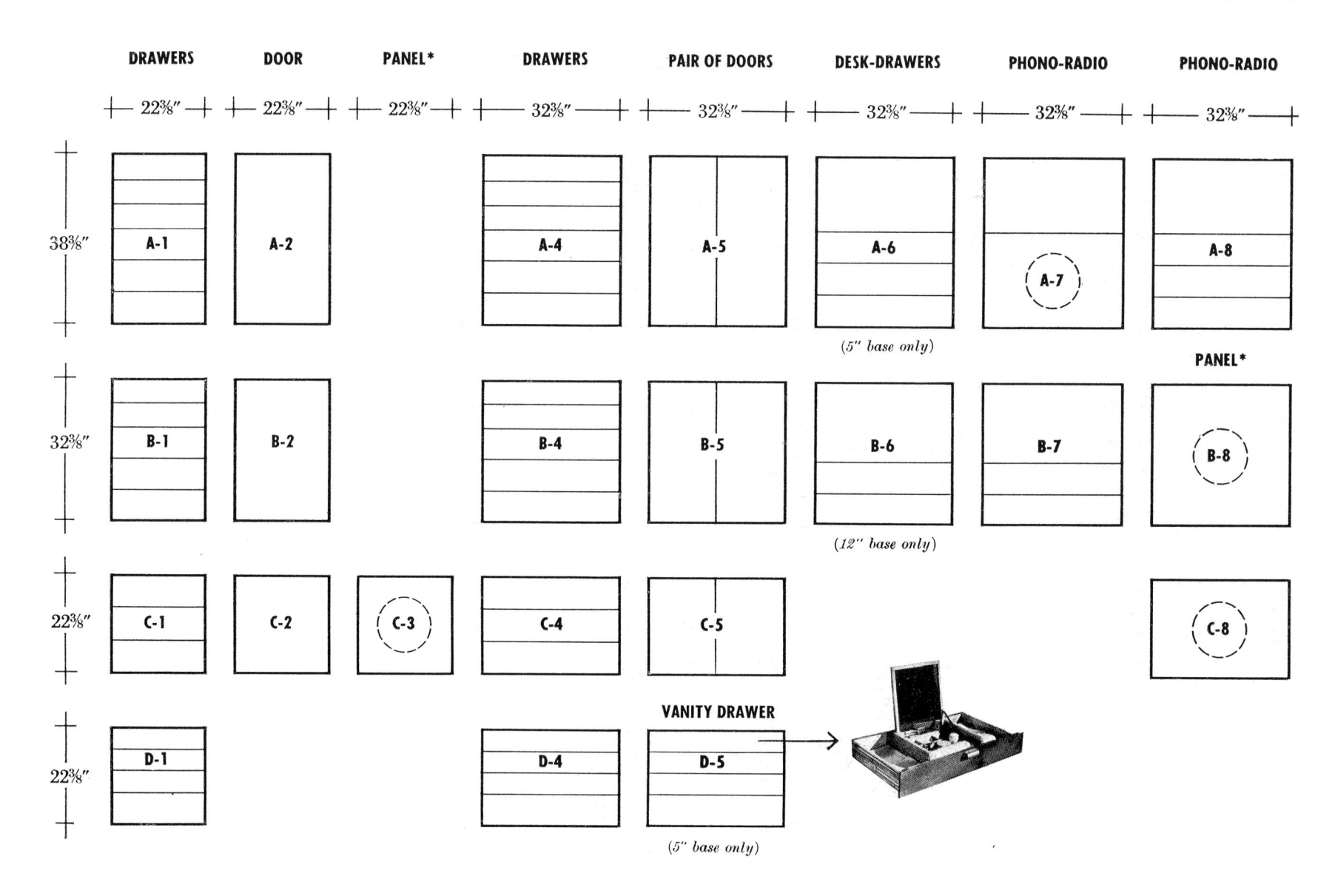

	DRAWERS	DOOR	PANEL*	DRAWERS	PAIR OF DOORS	DESK-DRAWERS	PHONO-RADIO	PHONO-RADIO
	22⅜"	22⅜"	22⅜"	32⅜"	32⅜"	32⅜"	32⅜"	32⅜"
38⅜"	A-1	A-2		A-4	A-5	A-6	A-7	A-8
						(5" base only)		PANEL*
32⅜"	B-1	B-2		B-4	B-5	B-6	B-7	B-8
							(12" base only)	
22⅜"	C-1	C-2	C-3	C-4	C-5			C-8
22⅜"	D-1			D-4	D-5 VANITY DRAWER			
					(5" base only)			

BSC components have been arranged in the typical combinations illustrated in order to fit nine standard grid openings. The Herman Miller Furniture Company supplies basic component inserts only. The frame should be produced locally, by a mill or cabinet maker; in many instances it is built by the contractor on the job (see page 25).

DRAWERS are finished complete with pulls and flush wood side slides which attach directly to the inside of the frame (see page 25). For single drawers see page 30. The special vanity drawer (see cut) is equipped with extension slides and fold-down mirror.

DOORS are furnished with pulls and pin hinges. When ordering "pairs of doors" specify pulls "top," "bottom" or "center." When ordering single doors specify, in addition, hinges "left" or "right" (facing).

DESK LIDS are furnished with pulls and lid supports, and are hinged to an inner platform. Also included are pigeonhole unit (ebonized only) and desk light (see page 26). Desk-drawer units should be placed on the appropriate base indicated in chart, to insure proper writing height.

RADIO-PHONOGRAPH inserts include drop lid (complete with pull and lid supports), turntable slide with blank mounting board, blank radio face panel and concealed center divider with shelf for chassis. Provide for proper ventilation. (See also page 26.)

DRAWERS	PAIR OF DOORS	DESK-DRAWERS	PHONO-RADIO-SPEAKER	PHONO-RADIO-DRAWERS	PANEL*	SPECIAL PANEL
⊢— 38⅜" —⊣	⊢— 38⅜" —⊣	⊢— 38⅜" —⊣	⊢— 38⅜" —⊣	⊢— 38⅜" —⊣	⊢— 38⅜" —⊣	⊢— up to 80" —⊣
A-9	A-10	A-11	A-12	A-13	A-14	A-15
		(5" base only)				+ specify +
B-9	B-10	B-11		B-13	B-14	B-15
		(12" base only)				+ specify +
C-9	C-10				C-14	C-15
						+ specify +
D-9						

ALL DIMENSIONS INCLUDE NECESSARY CLEARANCES

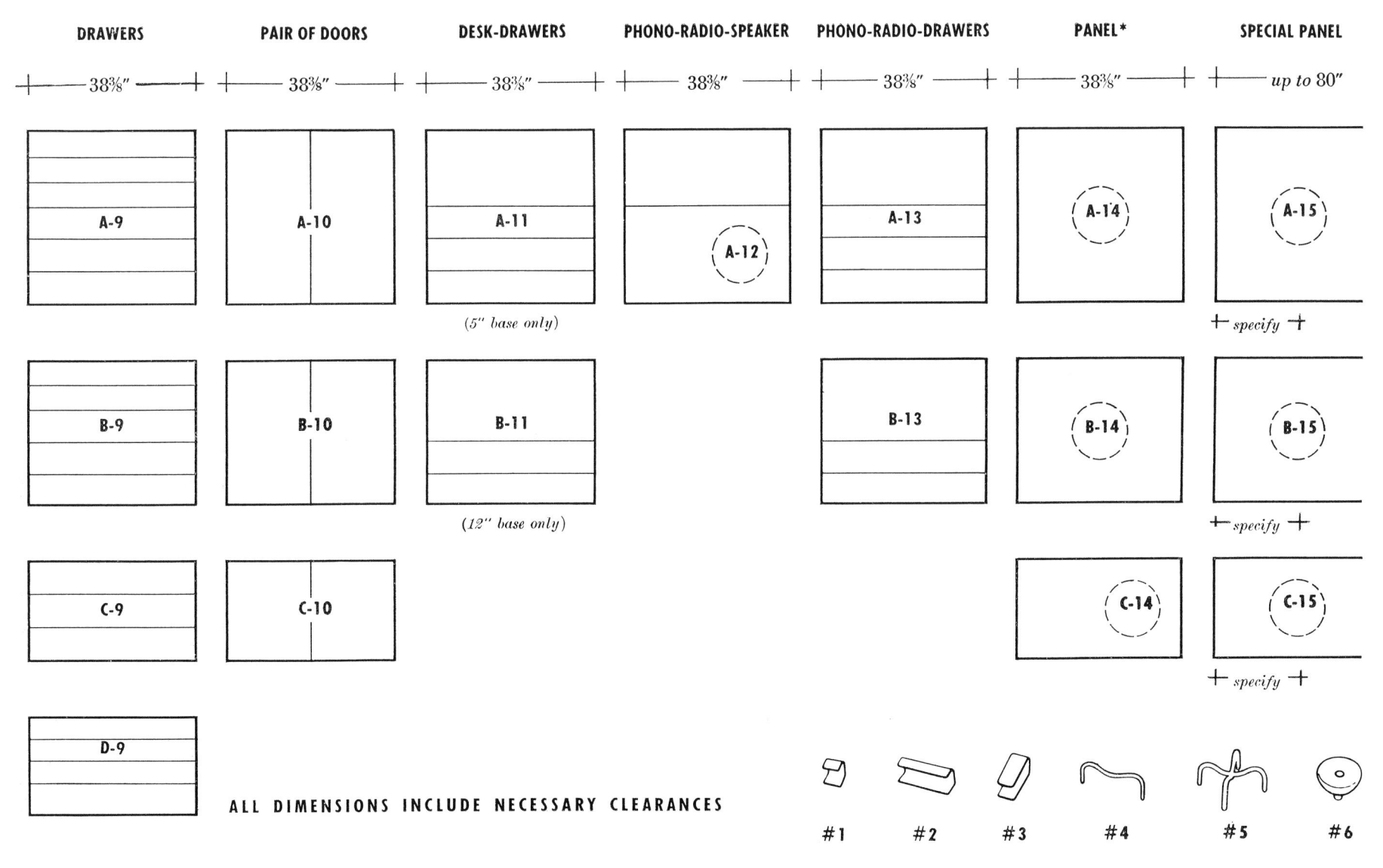

#1   #2   #3   #4   #5   #6

TELEVISION may be built into a BSC wall by making the necessary cutouts in a standard "panel." BSC structure should be made deep enough to accommodate tube. Provide proper ventilation.

PANELS are available to fill in blank spaces on BSC installations where both faces are exposed. If ordered as **SPEAKER PANELS** they are furnished with 13½" dia. opening for 15" speaker, and flush cloth insert.

SPECIAL PANELS are available in three heights, and may be ordered in any length up to 80". They are used to fill in spaces which do not conform to the standard grid openings. (See also pages 24 and 25.) When ordered as **SPECIAL SPEAKER PANELS** they will be furnished with the standard speaker opening and cloth insert. Diagram indicates how position of speaker opening should be specified.

PULLS are chrome-plated and identical in design and quality with those used on all Herman Miller furniture. Pulls 1, 2 and 3 form a related group, as do pulls 4 and 5. (Do not use pull 5 except on large doors.) Pull 6 is a wood knob with a chrome-plated insert. The finish always matches the front to which the pull is applied. #1 pull is standard for all desk and radio-phonograph droplids.

STANDARD FINISHES of inserts include Tawny Walnut (TW), Chili Walnut (CW), Comb Grain Oak (CGO), Ebonized (E), Bittersweet Red (BR), Forest Green (FG) and Gunmetal (GM).

The nine basic Herman Miller drawers are individually obtainable for special installations which require arrangements different from those shown on master chart (pages 28 and 29). Consult diagram at right for sizes and order numbers. All dimensions include necessary clearances, so that heights of drawer fronts may simply be added up to get over-all height of entire stack. Drawers are finished complete with pulls (see page 29) and flush wood slides, which attach directly to the sides of the frame and stop the drawer when closed. All drawers fit a minimum depth of 18½" (see page 25). Special vanity drawer is shown on page 28, and is the same size as "DS-532" in chart below. When using this unit, special care should be taken to install it at the proper height, leaving sufficient knee space below vanity drawer.

	22⅜"	32⅜"	38⅜"
7 7/16"	DS-722	DS-732	DS-738
6"	DS-622	DS-632	DS-638
5"	DS-522	DS-532	DS-538

QUESTIONS AND ANSWERS ON BSC

Q Are the sizes of drawers, doors, etc., given in the chart exact or do they include necessary clearances?
A They include necessary clearances.

Q How are the drawers hung?
A The drawers are provided with simple wood slides that are nailed to the frame. See page 25 for details.

Q Do you supply masonite for the back panels on free-standing BSC walls?
A No. Only finished plywood panels are offered. We suggest obtaining masonite locally.

Q Does Herman Miller furnish framing details to its customers if a rough sketch is given them?
A Details should not be needed if the BSC section is studied carefully. However, a consulting service is available. Inquiries on any phase of BSC design should be addressed to the company's New York showroom at 1 Park Avenue.

Q Does Herman Miller supply bases for BSC units?
A No. It is more economical to cut a piece of wood to size on the job.

Q Do you supply the framework for BSC installations?
A No. Since each installation is different it is impossible to give to the purchaser the advantages of factory production. Local fabrication is equally satisfactory and more economical.

Q What is the best type of wood to use for the framework?
A The best material is 13/16" plywood. See page 25 of this booklet.

Q Do you supply counter tops when low units are specified?
A No.

Q Can I supply Herman Miller with my own hardware?
A No. However, BSC components may be ordered without hardware if purchaser wishes to apply his own.

Q Are special wood finishes available?
A Yes, at an additional charge of 15%. Special finishes are available on our standard Walnut and Comb Grain Oak Veneers only. A large sample of desired finish should be submitted to Herman Miller Furniture Co. Solid lacquer colors can also be matched.

Q Do the arrangements shown on pages 28 and 29 come already pre-assembled?
A No. The components have to be fitted into the framework on the job.

Q How does one fasten blank panels and speaker panels to the framework?
A Past procedure has been to install a cleat behind the panel and to fasten the panel with exposed screws. Oval head chromium-plated screws with screw washers present the best appearance.

Q Does Herman Miller supply the radios, etc., for BSC installations?
A No. Our showrooms, however, are available for consultation on problems of radio, television, etc.

Facing page: A typical installation of BSC components in a double-faced room divider.

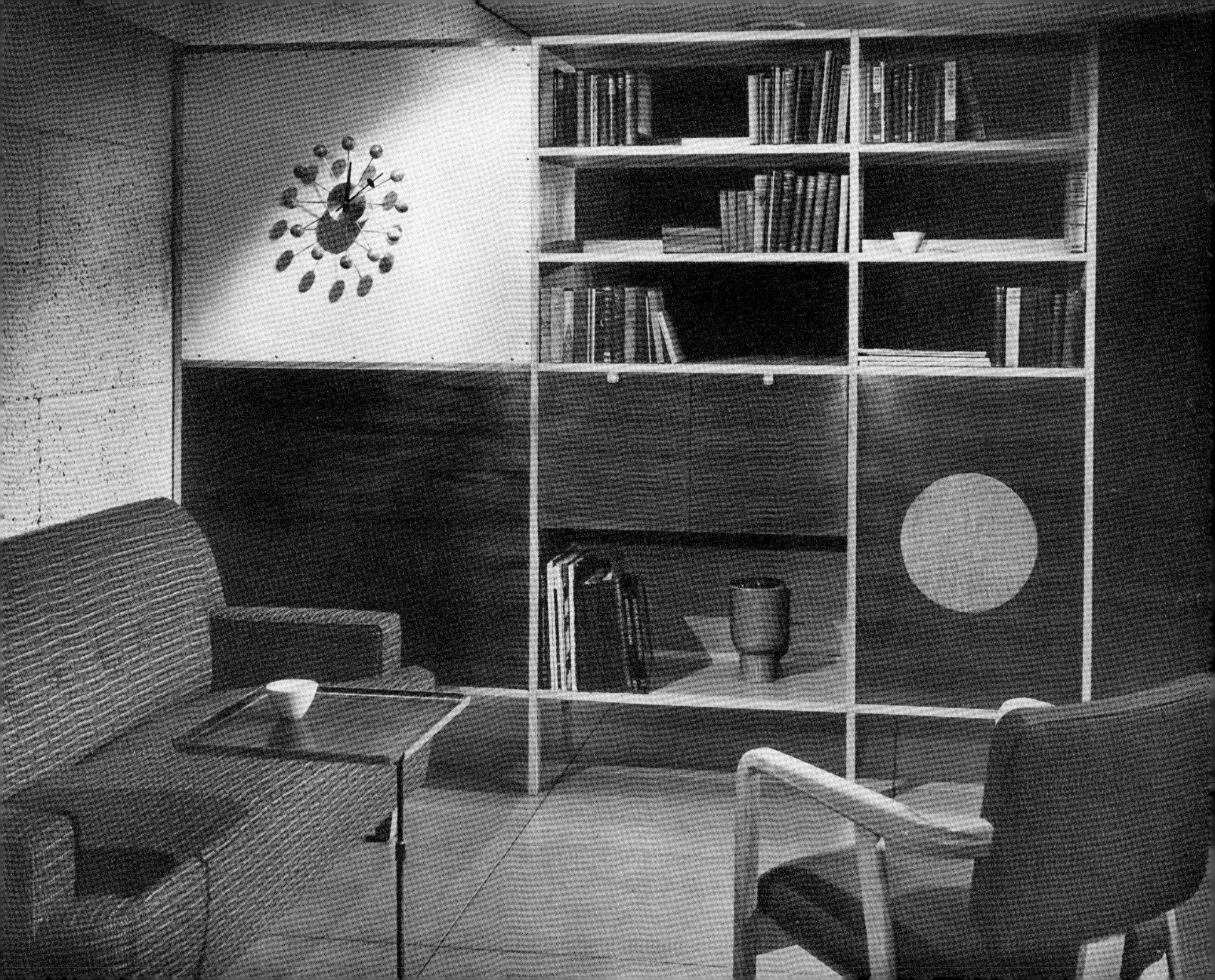

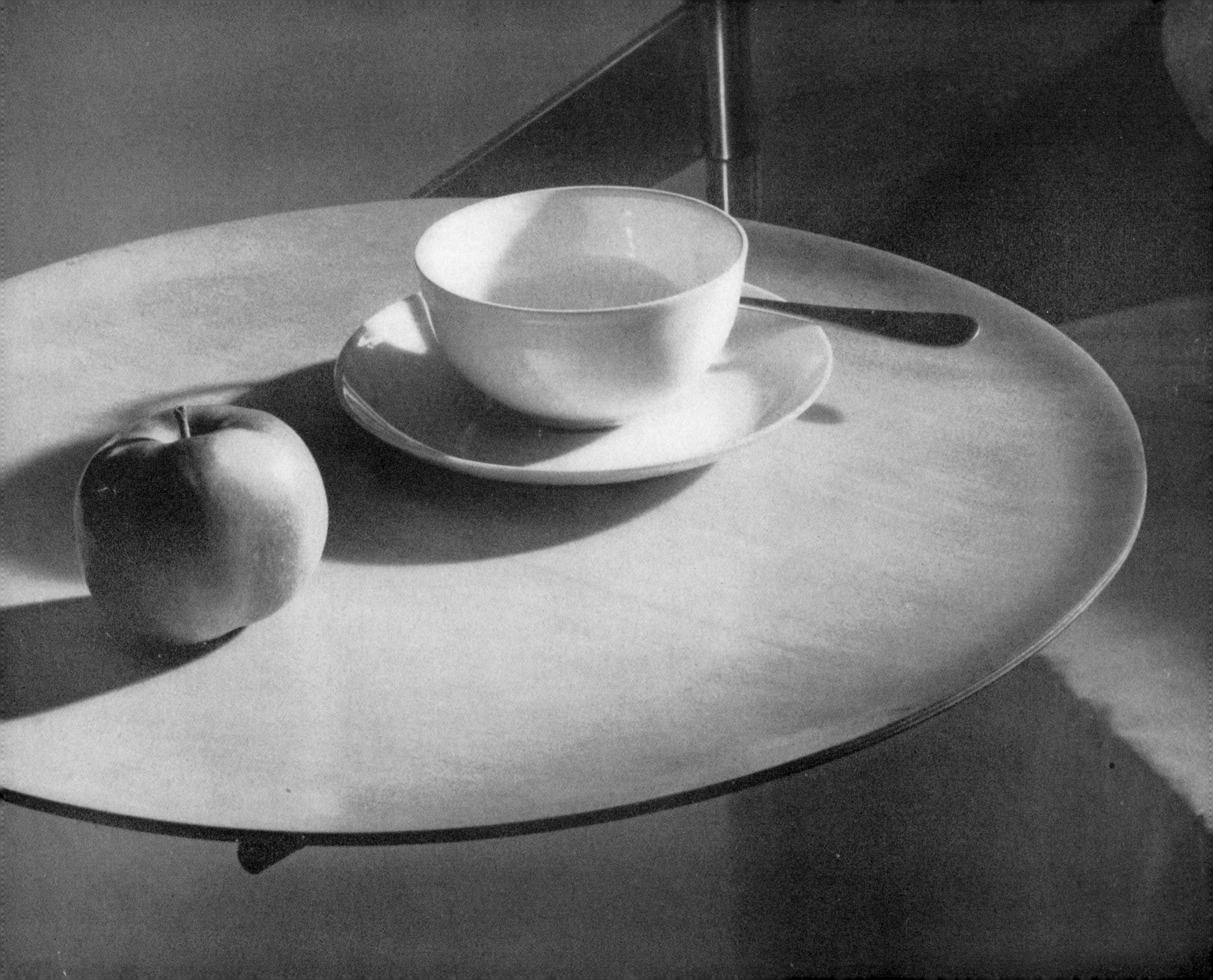

sleeping

Furniture for the contemporary bedroom has changed its composition greatly in the past half-dozen years. Except for the most retarded end of the market, the bedroom "suite" has become obsolete—housewives have become impatient with the task of cleaning small rooms occupied by seven to ten separate pieces of furniture, and the logical elimination process has gone on to the point where the modern bedroom consists of little more than the beds, a light chair, bedside units and the necessary storage. Apparatus for sleeping and dressing in the Herman Miller Collection carries the expression of this trend as far as it can be done in terms of movable units, and it is completely in keeping with the design requirements of the contemporary bed-dressing room interior.

4909-U *bed,* **4615** *bedside tables*

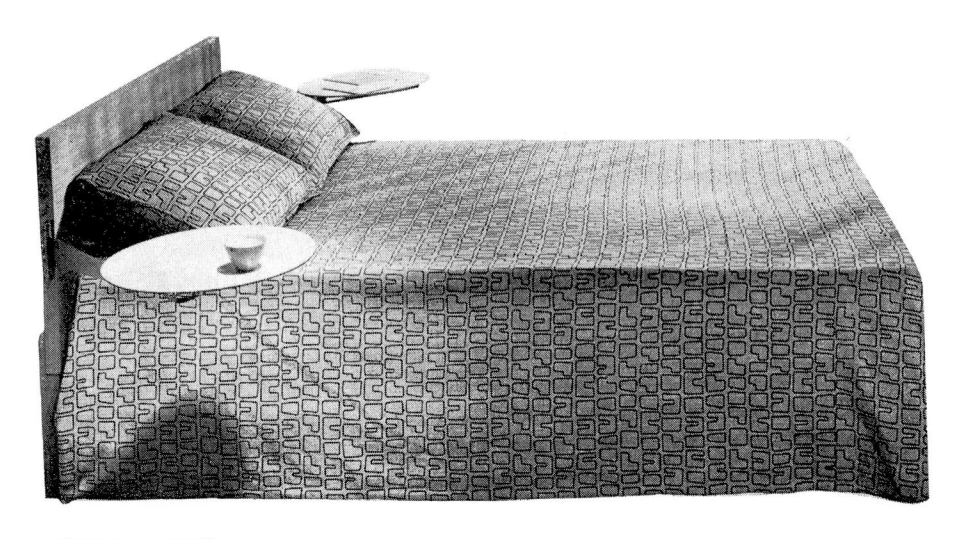

4908 *bed,* **4952** *trays*

4649-D *headboard*
4618 *bedside table*

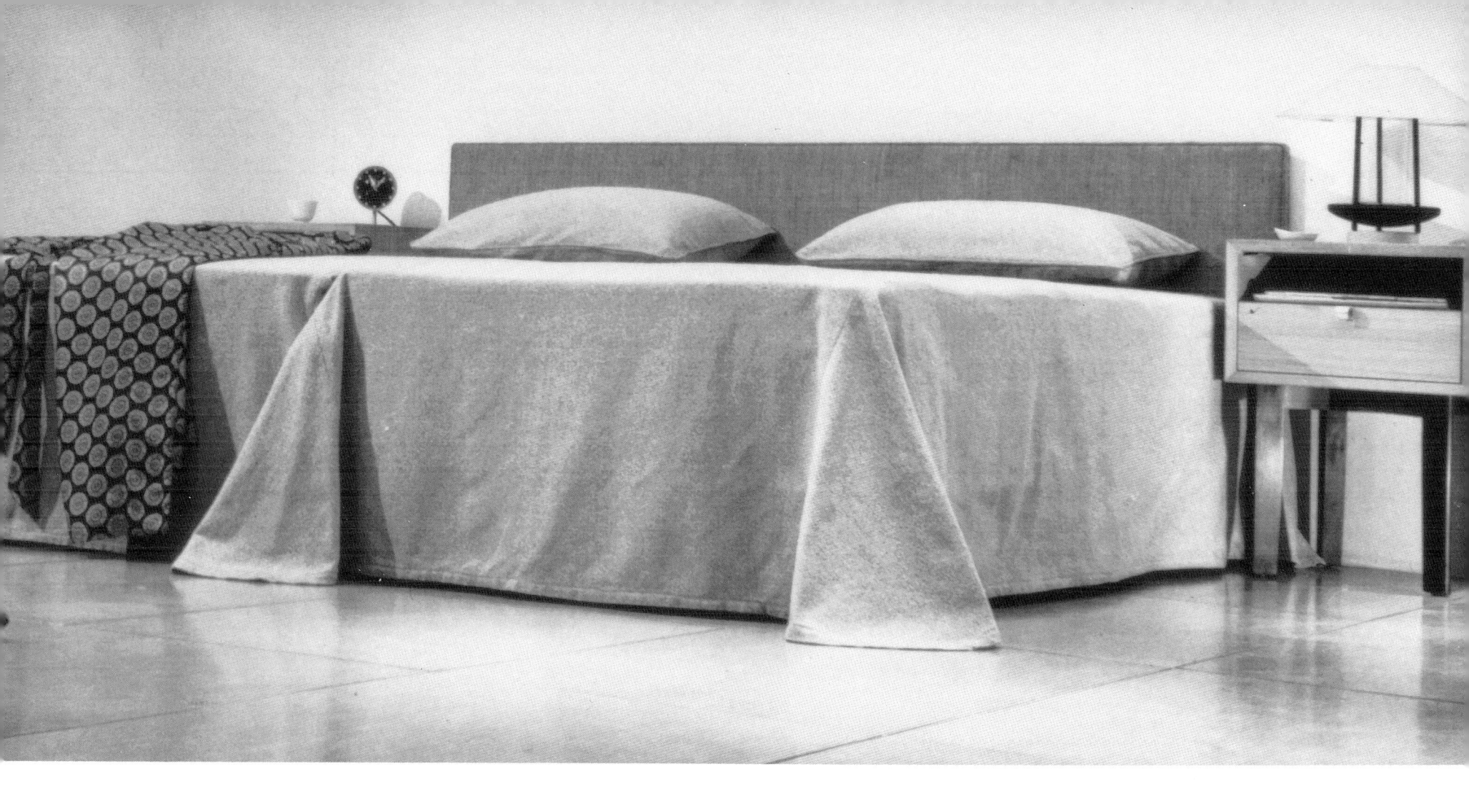

BEDS: 79" headboard attached to swing-out twin-size steel bedframes: 4909-U (upholstered, see above), 4909 (veneered). 54" headboard attached to steel bedframe on casters: 4908-U (upholstered), 4908 (veneered, see facing page). 39" versions: 4907-U (upholstered) and 4907 (veneered). Standard wood finishes (no lacquer). 4649-D, 19"x54" wall-hung cane headboard for use with any standard box spring and mattress on legs. Birch finished to match standard wood finishes, natural cane (see facing page). Twin size: 4649 (19"x38").
BEDSIDE TABLES: 4615 (above) 17$\frac{13}{16}$" wide, 24" over-all high, 18½" deep. Standard wood finishes, legs ebonized or matching. 4618 (facing page) and 4617 (right): Same over-all dimensions, 5½" legs, all standard wood finishes. Specify door hinged right (RHF) or left (LHF) facing. 4952, 18" dia. molded plywood bed trays on brushed chrome double-swing-out supports attached to edge of headboard. Walnut, Comb Grain Oak or Birch (see facing page). Specify right or left (facing).

4617

4709-L *bedside unit*
4646 *storage headbds.*

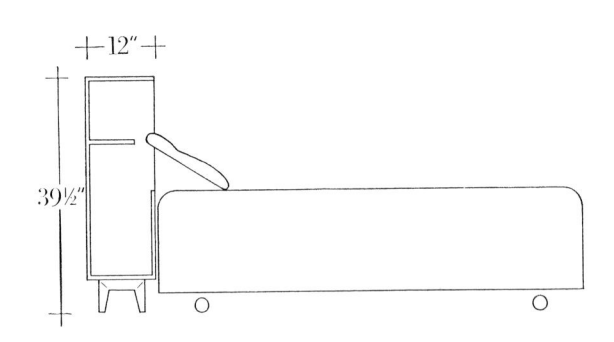

Storage headboards may be used with twin or full-size bedding up to 14" in height. Steel bedframes on casters (H-2) are equipped with swing hinges for fastening to the units. The padded headrest (covered in woven textiles or plastic fabric) can be set at any desired angle and is individually adjustable in double bed models. Matching nightstands with pull-out shelf: 4608 (17" wide) and 4708 (24" wide). The 24" unit may be fitted with swing-out bedside lamps (4708-L), a tilt-front radio panel (4709) or both (4709-L, see facing page). Swing-out lamps have a dull grey enamel housing with frosted glass front. Radio equipment is not furnished: purchaser is to make cut-out in blank face and may install any small table set. Space behind headrests has been designed for seasonal storage of blankets; books may be conveniently kept on the inside shelf. 4647-L and 4647-R combine headboard and bedside unit in one piece. All standard wood finishes, 5½" legs.

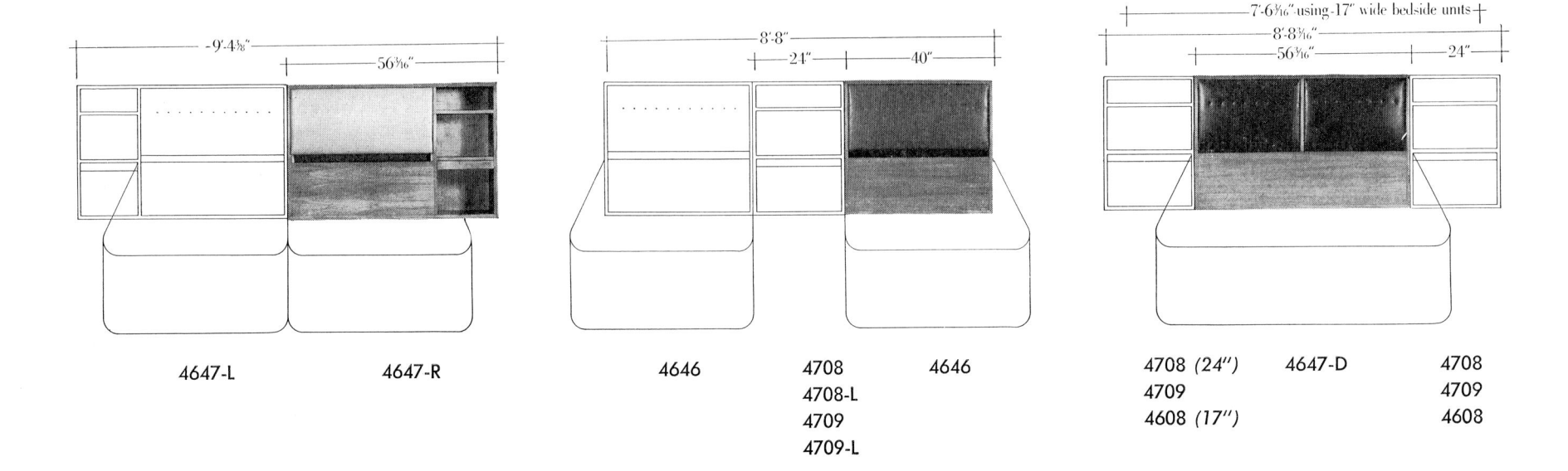

4647-L   4647-R

4646   4708
        4708-L
        4709
        4709-L

4708 (24")   4647-D   4708
4709   4709
4608 (17")   4608

36

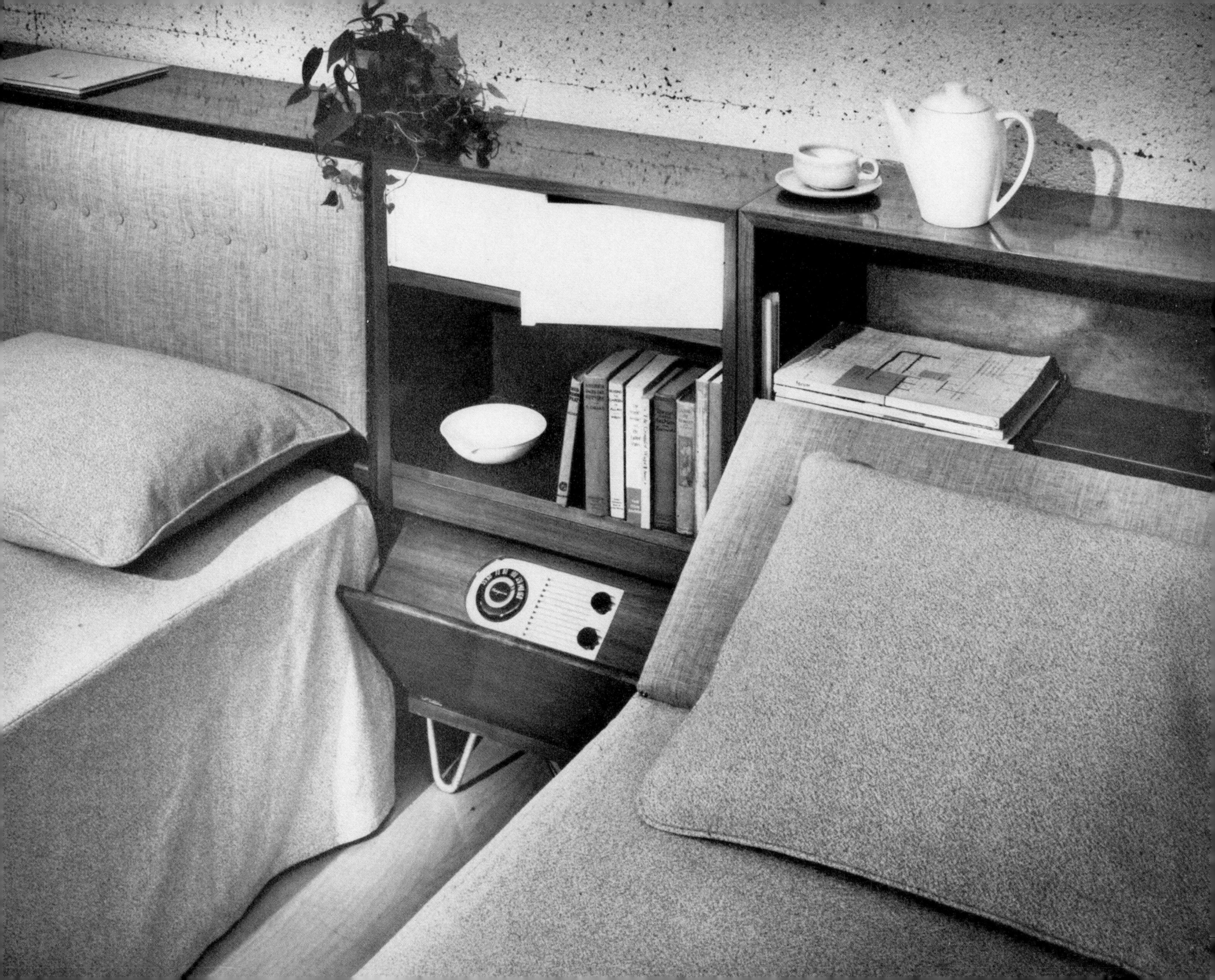

4901 *case*
4672 *seat*
4992 *bench*

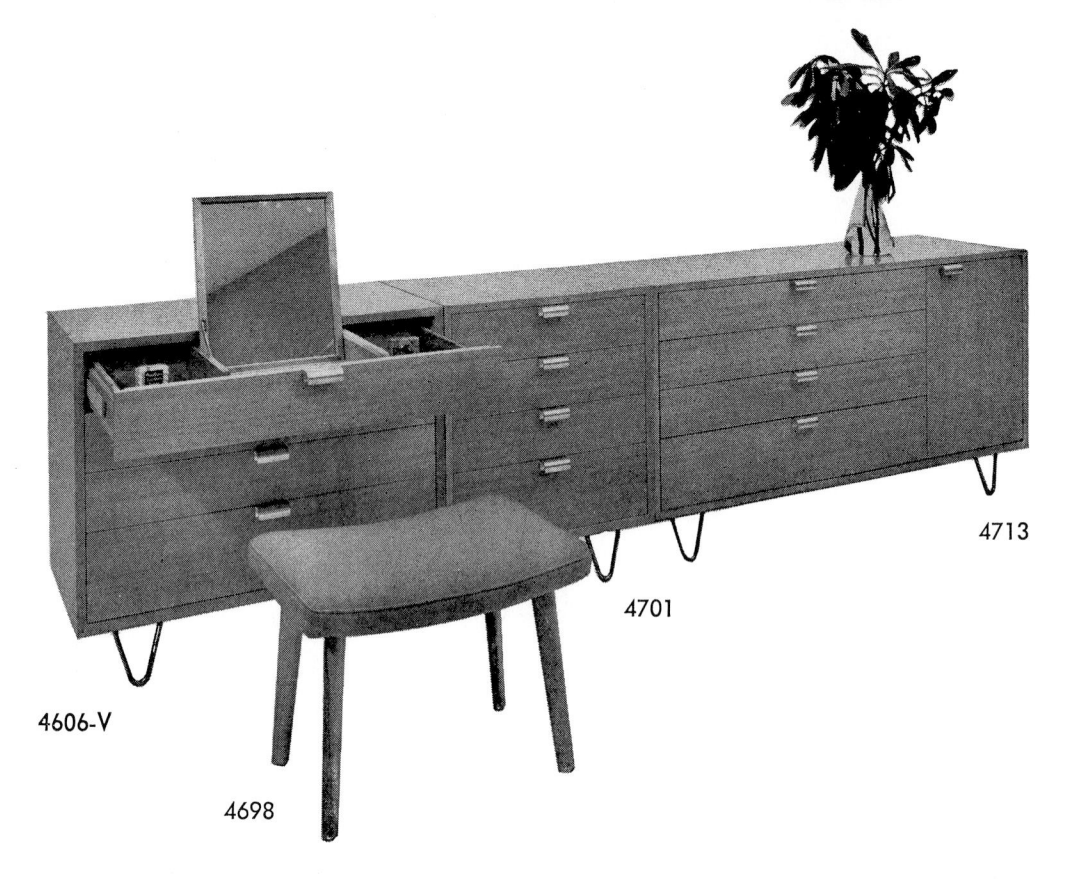

4606-V chest (above), 24″ x 34″, 18½″ deep, has a vanity drawer on extension slides. 4661 suspended vanity (right) is 30″ wide and may be used only between 24″ high, 18½″ deep cases on 5½″ legs. It contains a lift-up mirror, fluorescent light and cosmetic compartments. 4901 guestroom unit (facing page), 24″ x 57 3/16″, 18½″ deep, combines storage with drop-leaf pull-out desk and vanity drawer. All standard wood finishes, for use on 14″ high platform benches only. See also pp. 16-17.

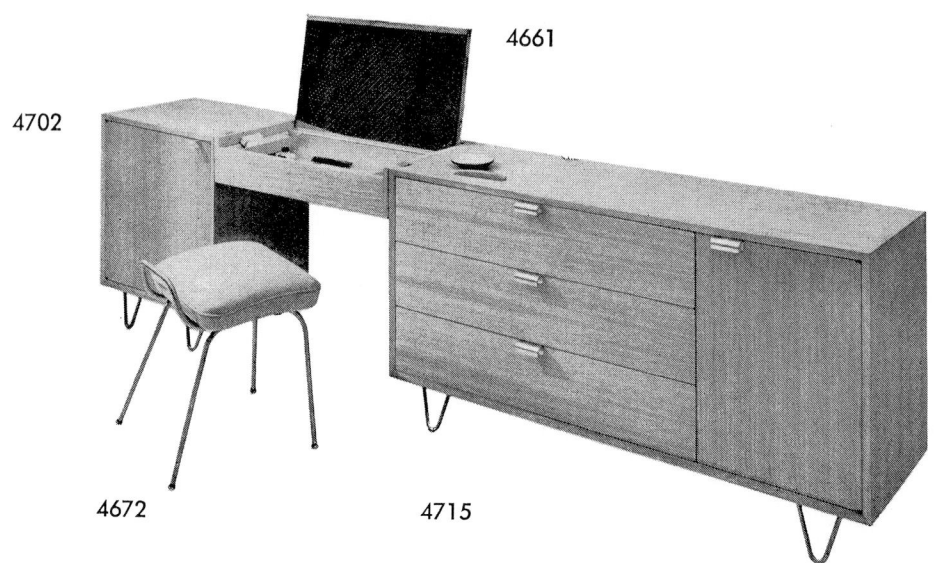

38

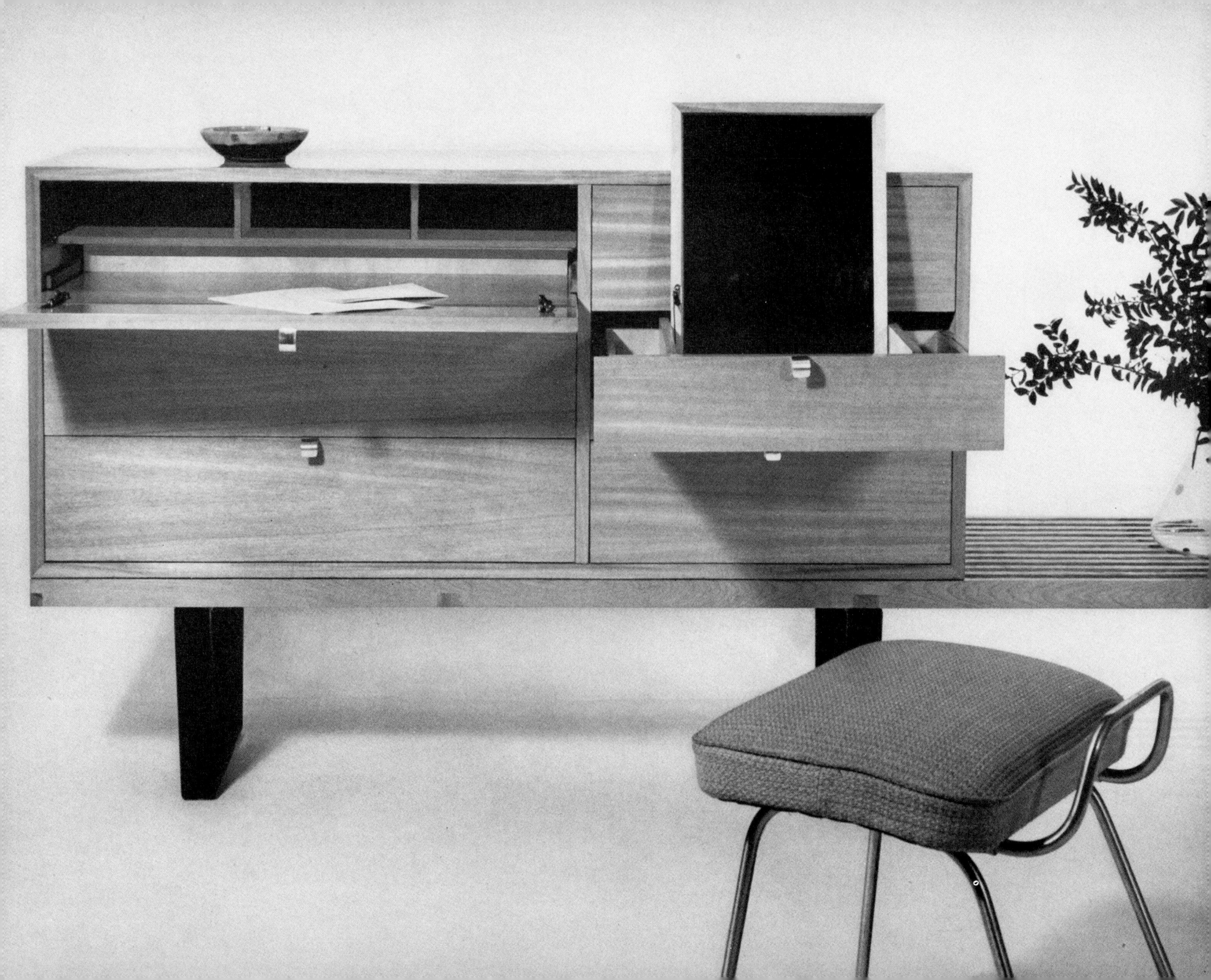

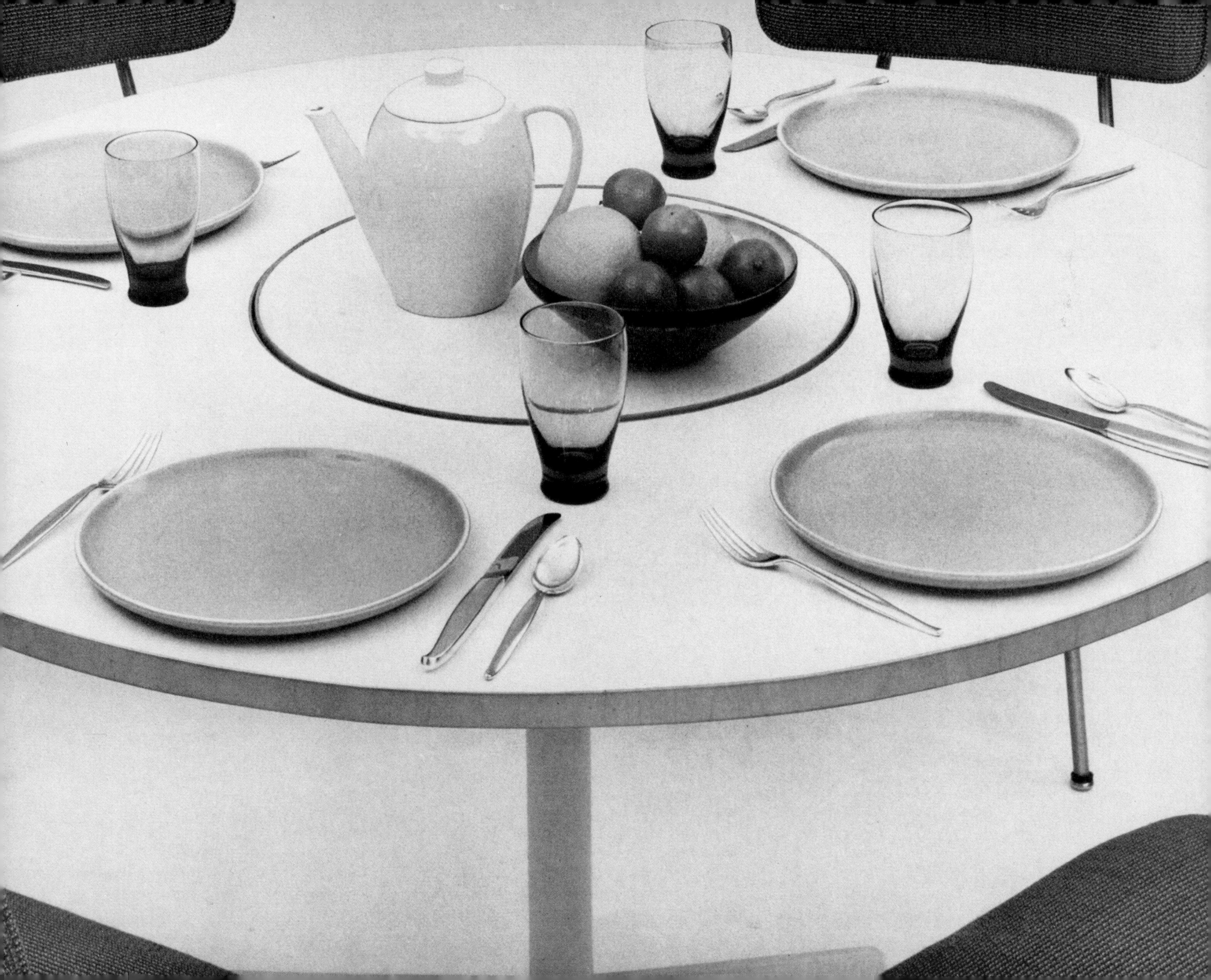

dining

Dining, more than any other family activity, requires the utmost flexibility in design. The rapid disappearance of the dining room as a special and separate space has taken with it a good deal of the old formality; also, the necessity of using general living space for dining has changed the character of the furniture. As spaces become multi-purpose, so does the furniture. Hence there is today no "ideal" type of dining table, since requirements vary too widely. And for the same reason, accessory pieces such as sideboards and buffets work most effectively if they are also designed for use in general living areas. Seating is also affected by present-day circumstances, since the dining chair is expected to function equally well at a desk or as an occasional extra seating piece.

8430-X *table*
84" l.   30" w.   28½" h.
other sizes 7230-X — 72" l. x 30" w.
7830-X — 78" l. x 30" w.
8436-X — 84" l. x 36" w.

4671 *chairs*

5021 *48" dia.   29" h.*

5021 lazy-susan table (above), has flush center turn table, seats six. Top is surfaced with hard plastic (choice of five colors) and the edge is finished to match comb grain oak or any of the standard wood finishes. Cast metal base is available in dull white or black enamel. 8430-X table (facing page) seats eight. Top is one of the standard wood finishes or hard plastic (choice of five colors). The base can be had in brushed chrome, dull black or white enamel finish.

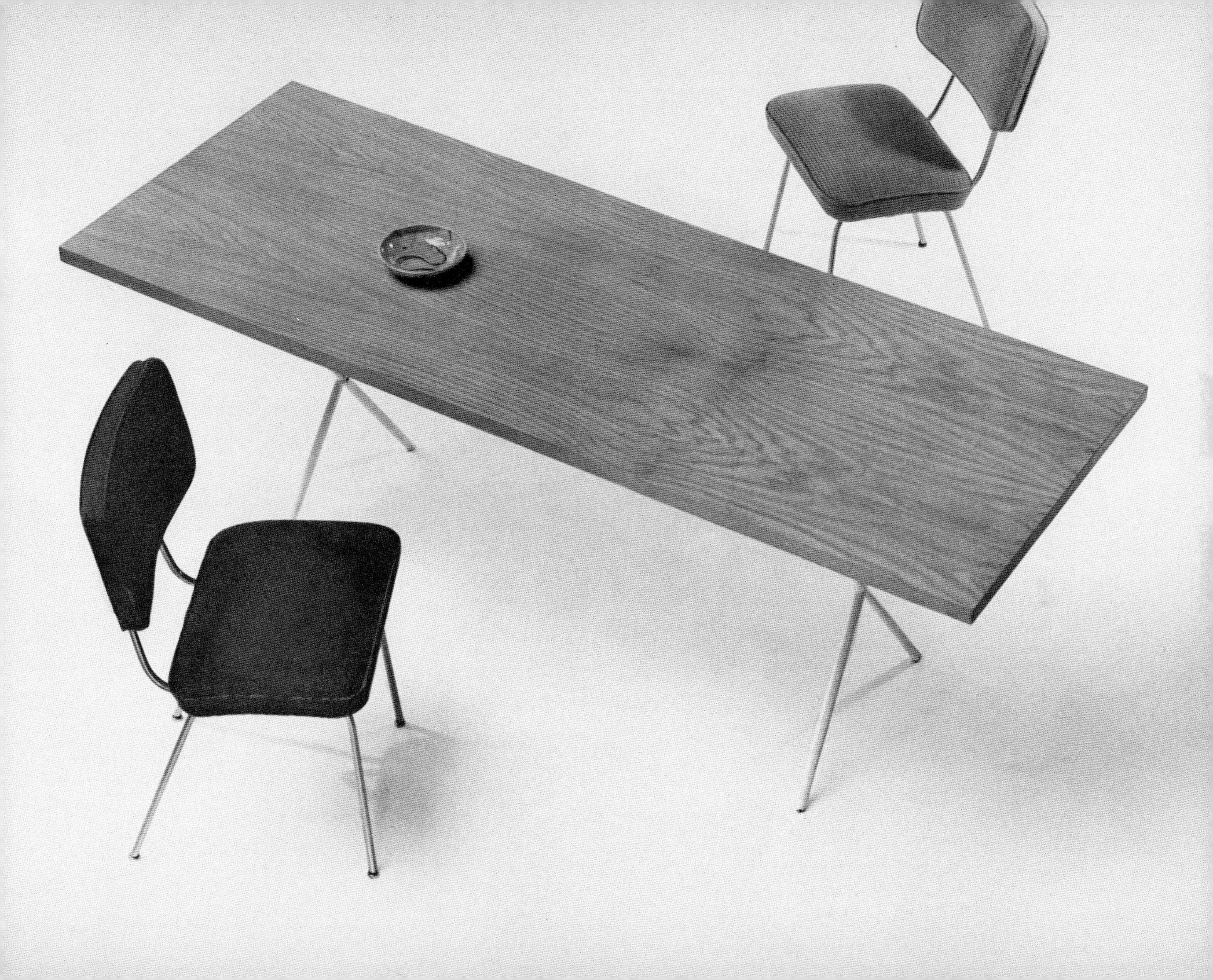

32 x 48

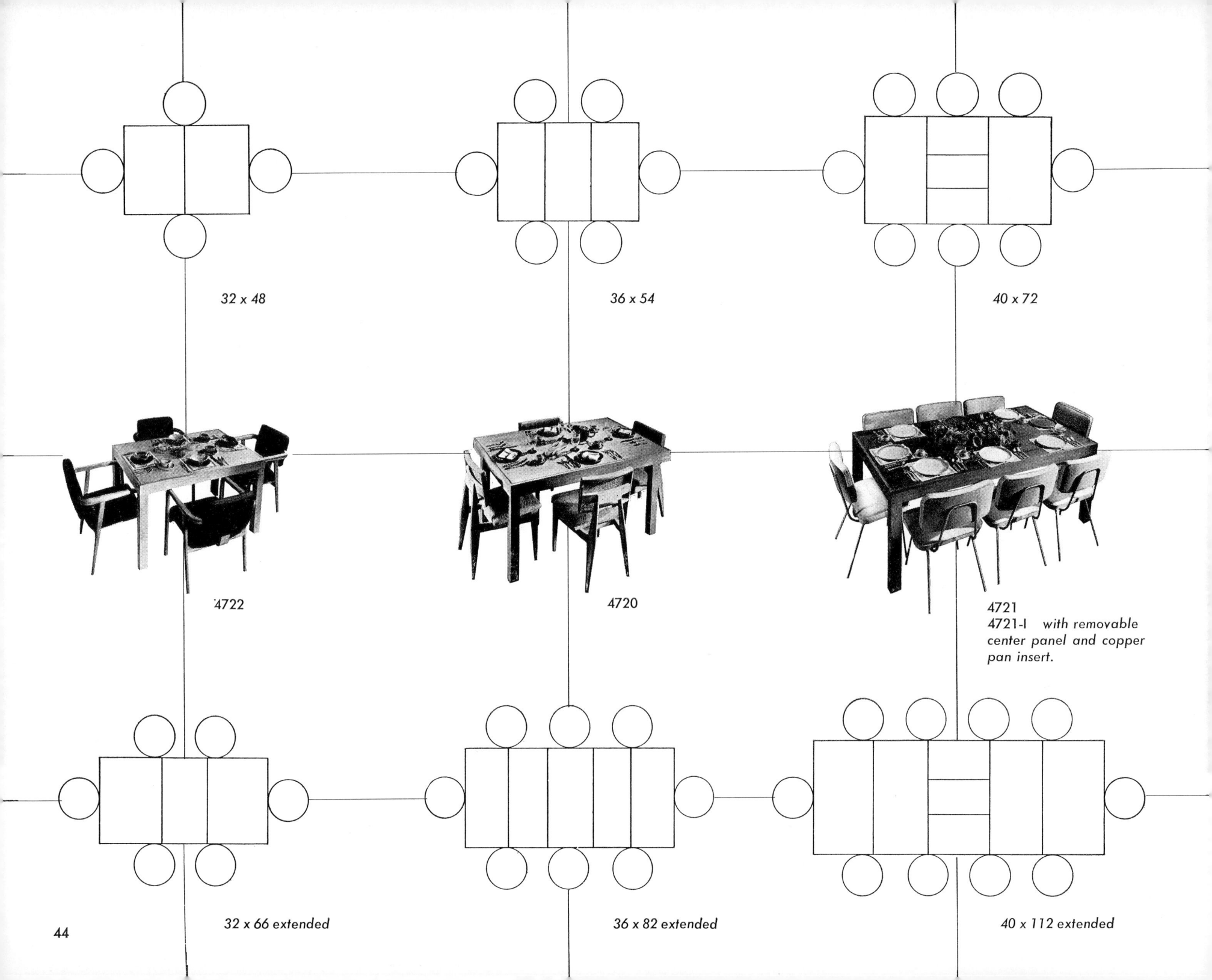

36 x 54

40 x 72

4722

4720

4721
4721-I with removable center panel and copper pan insert.

32 x 66 extended

36 x 82 extended

40 x 112 extended

4656 gateleg table (above), 18½" x 40" (closed), 29½" high, lines up with 24" cases on 5½" legs (see p. 16). Fully extended it seats eight generously (40" x 64⅞").

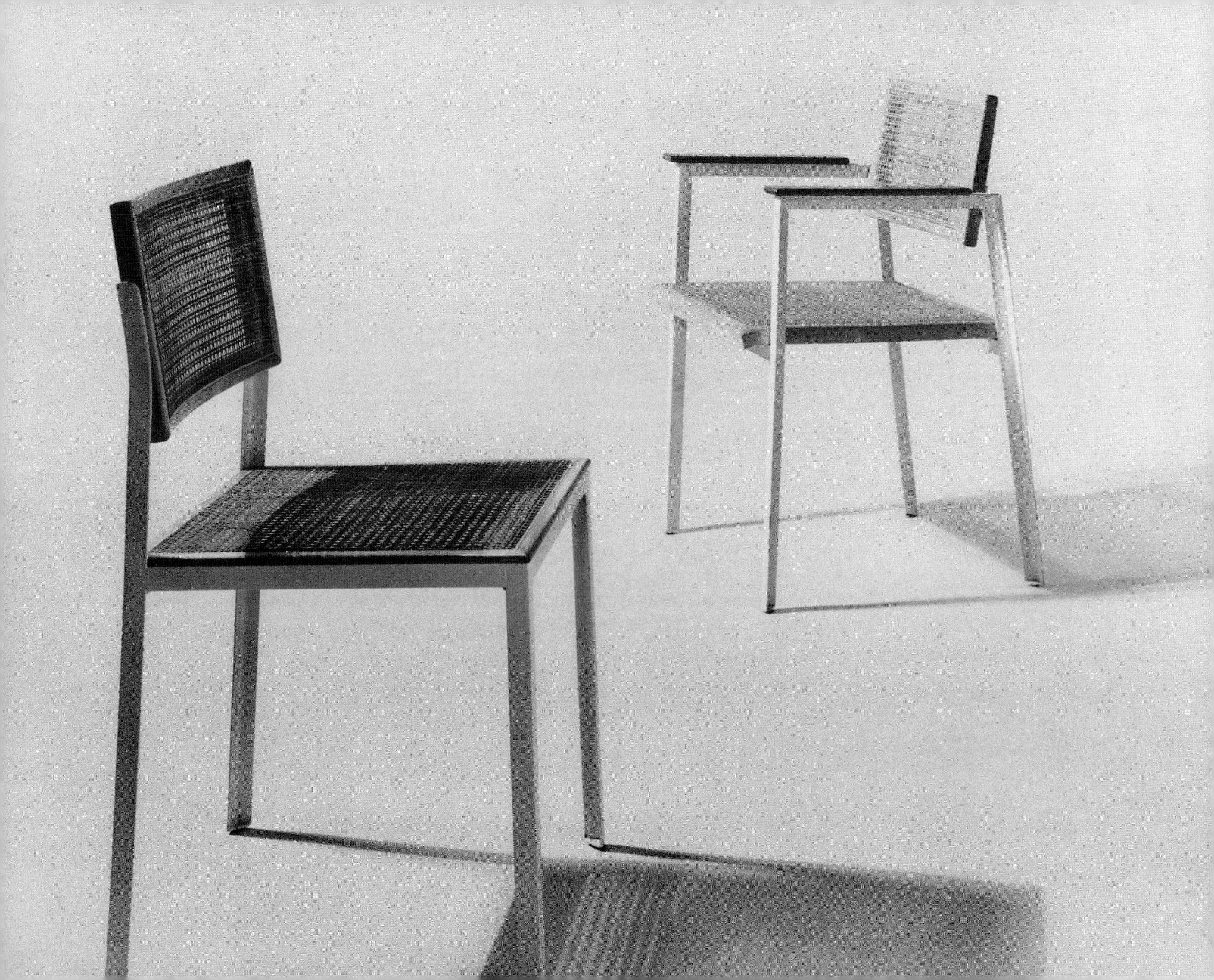

5068 *side chair 18″ w. 19½″ d. 32½″ h.*
5069 *arm chair 24½″ w. 21¾″ d. 32½″ h.*

5068 sidechair and 5069 armchair (facing page) Metal frame white or black enamel, seat and back natural cane in birch frames finished to match comb grain oak; same finish on armrests.
4671 sidechair (right), Constructed of aluminum rod which gives unusual resilience to the back; foam rubber on springs, satin aluminum finish.
4668 sidechair has upholstered seat and back and 4669 sidechair has upholstered seat and natural cane back. Birch frame finished to match standard wood finishes, foam rubber.

4669 *19″ w. 19″ d. 30″ h.*

4668 *19″ w. 19″ d. 30″ h.*

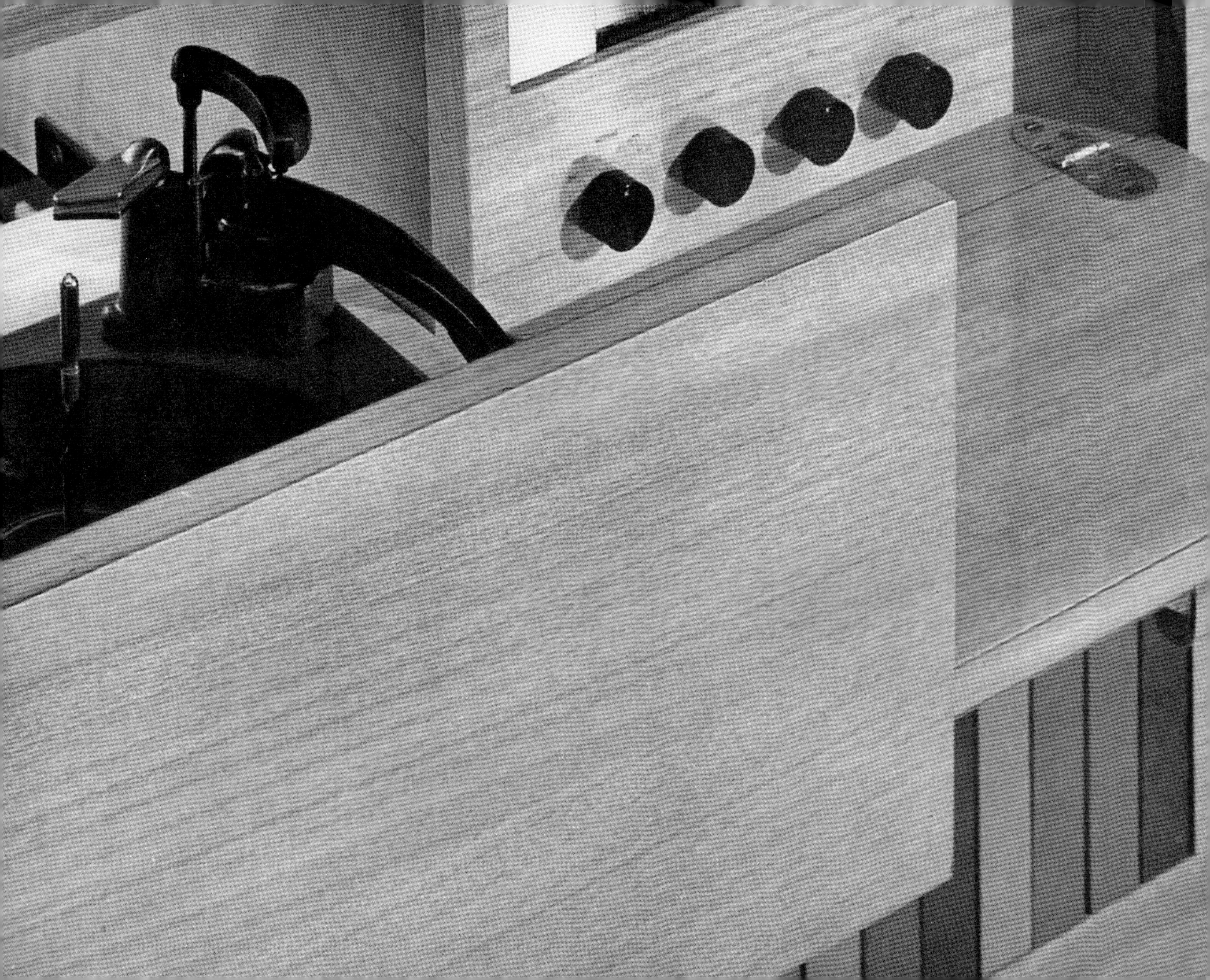

leisure

With the advent of radio, television, improved recordings, home movies and color slide projection, the amount of space needed for the machinery of family entertainment has vastly increased, a fact made evident in the preceding section on storage. Along with this development has come a corresponding change in seating, although a less noticeable one. Like the storage units, much soft seating has become "architectural" — that is, it lends itself to combinations which have the appearance of custom-made, built-in pieces. This trend is based on more than tastes in styling, for the furniture makes maintenance and housekeeping simpler. The pieces shown in this section cover a broad range of requirements and are executed in a wide variety of materials. Accessory pieces, including coffee tables, lamp tables, end tables and radio-television units are illustrated at the end of the section.

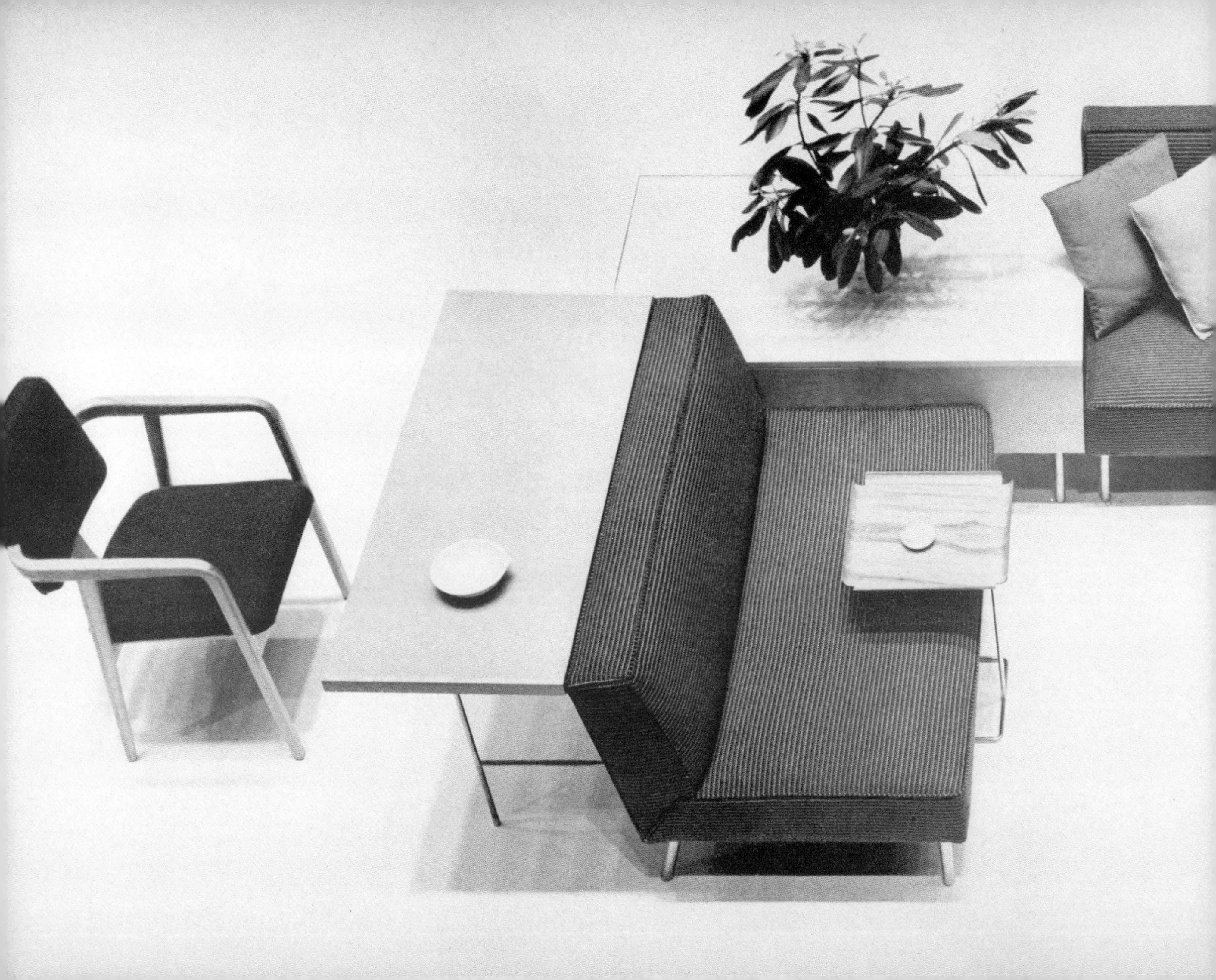

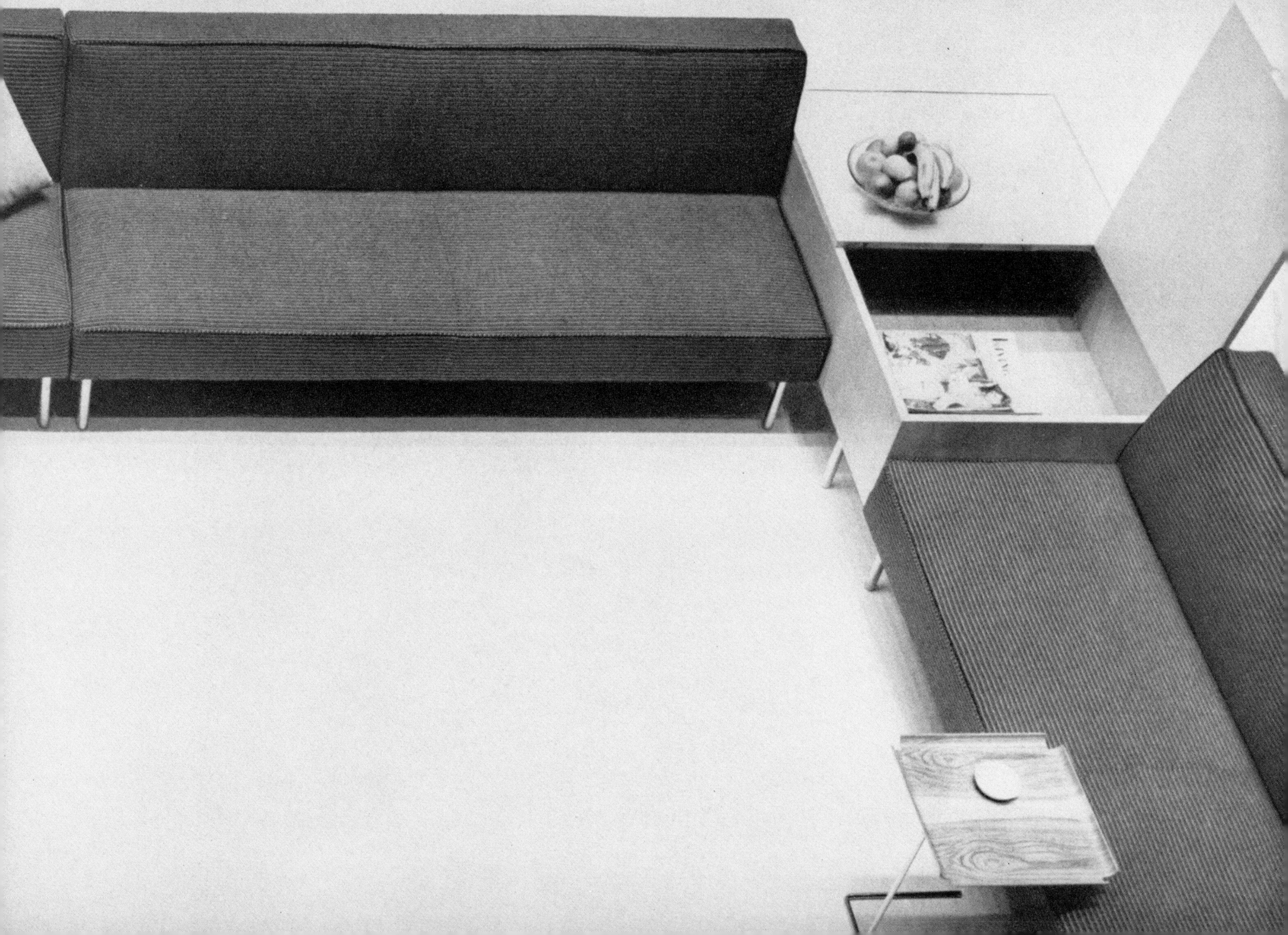

5056

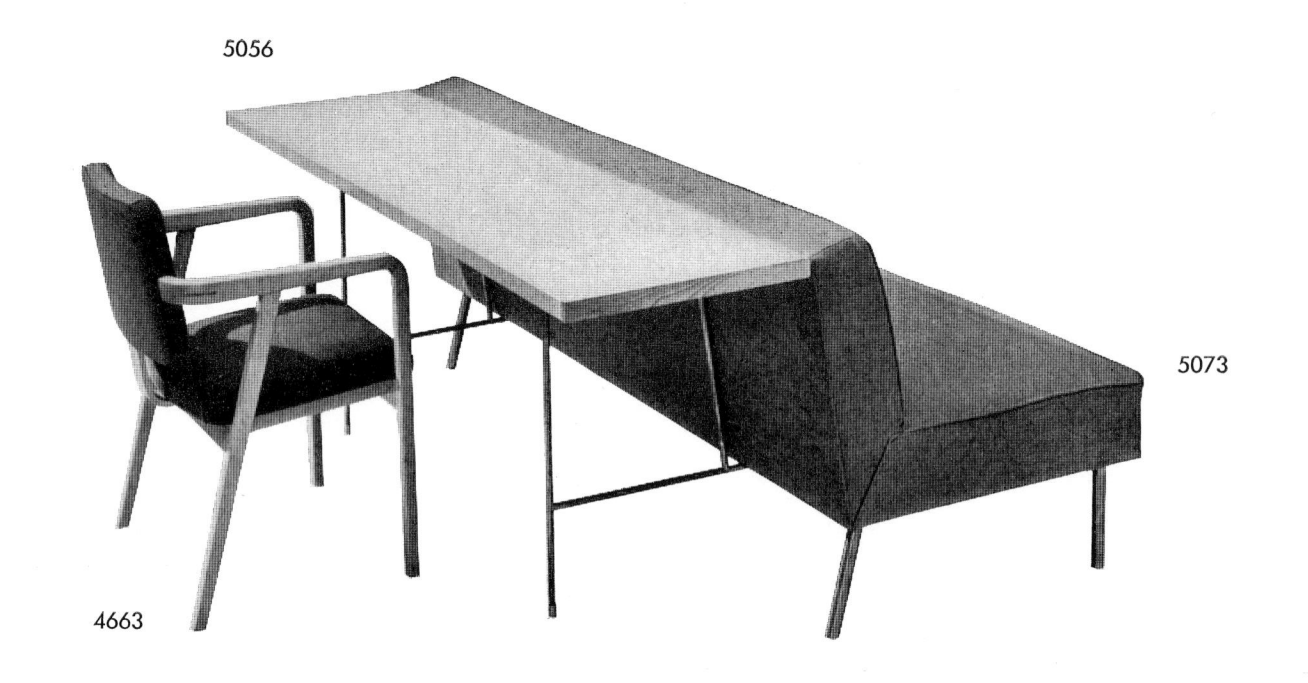

5073

4663

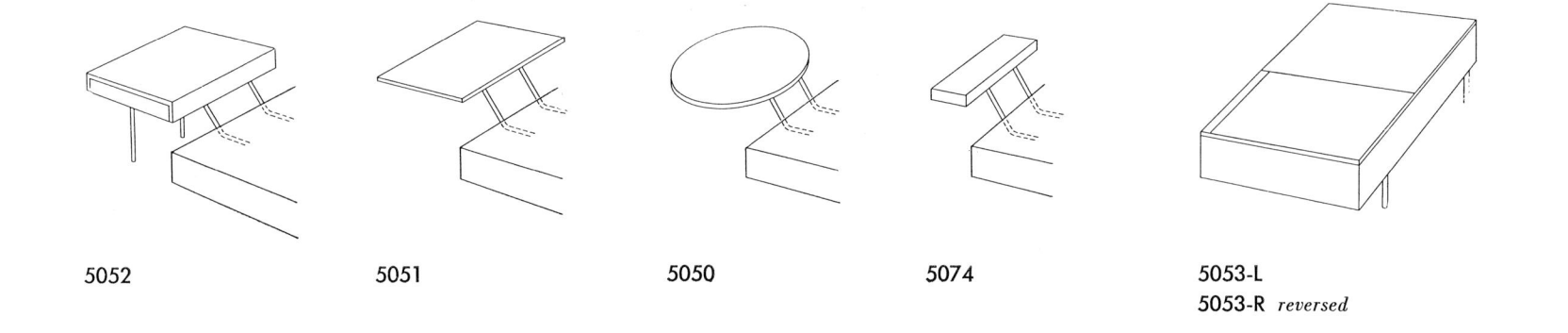

5052

5051

5050

5074

5053-L
5053-R *reversed*

52

5072 *(50" long)*   5071 *(25" long)*   5073 *(75" long)*   5070 *(25" x 32")*

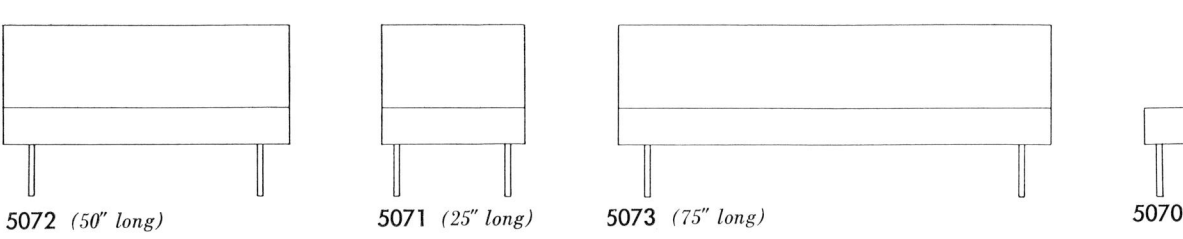

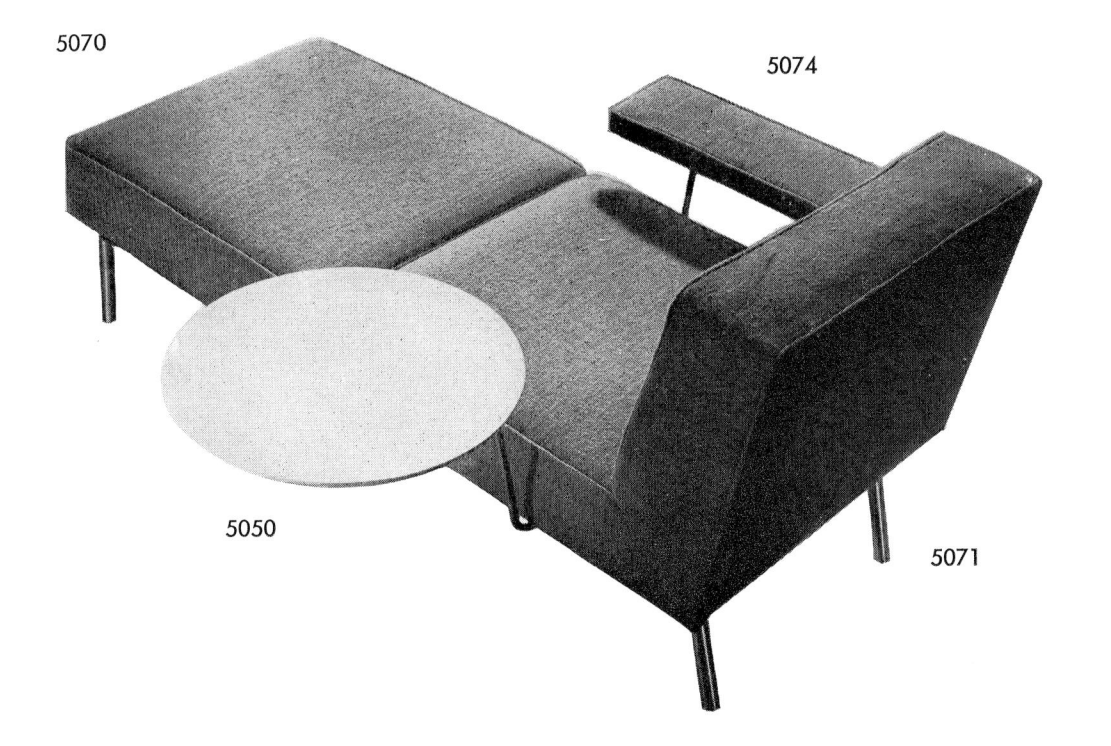

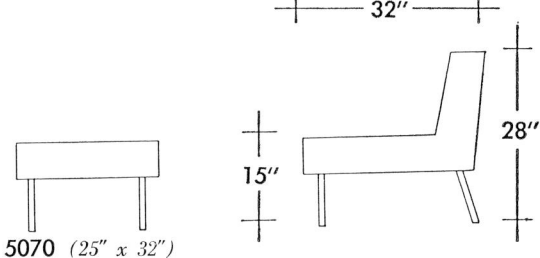

32" / 15" / 28"

5070
5074
5050
5071

The sectional seating units shown here and on preceding spread are constructed of foam rubber and springs, with legs of brushed chrome. The following components (facing page) may be attached to any of the above units or to the day bed which is shown on following spread:
5052 attached drawer-endtable, 15" x 23", birch shell, birch or white hard plastic top, brushed chrome supports with shoes for levelling.
5051 attached tray, 15" x 25", birch or white hard plastic top, brushed chrome supports.
5050 attached molded plywood tray, 18" dia., walnut, comb grain oak or birch, brushed chrome supports.
5074 attached upholstered armrest with tilting device, foam rubber, brushed chrome supports.
5053-L corner unit, 30" x 48", 20½" over-all high, with hinged lid. Birch shell, birch or white hard plastic top, brushed chrome legs.
5053-R reversed.
5056 attached back table, 20" wide, for use with 75" three-seater unit (5073). Top wrapped with plastic fabric, with birch ends in natural finish or stained to match any of the other standard wood finishes; legs brushed chrome, with shoes for levelling. 5054 is the 50" version for attachment to two-seater unit (5072).

5087 day bed, 33" x 75" (over-all), seat 15" high, back 27" over-all high. Removable bolsters of foam rubber, reversible foam rubber mattress on spring frame of natural birch; satin aluminum legs. If used in corner arrangement (right) 652 corner unit provides space for storage of blankets and may be augmented by 4742 chairside phonograph-radio cabinet (p. 68) or one of the chairside tables in the 4744 series (p. 64). Attachable components shown on page 52 may also be applied. Permanent cover on mattress and bolsters.
5087-T, same with mattress and bolsters covered in grey ticking only.
5087-Z, same with zip-on cover on mattress, permanent cover on bolsters.
The above three versions are also available for free-standing use with attached back support of natural birch (5088, 5088-T and 5088-Z, see cut below) and without back support or bolsters (5089, 5089-T and 5089-Z).

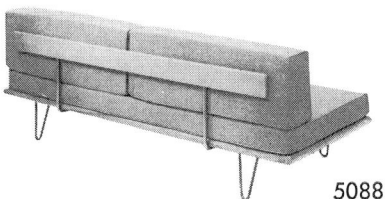

5088 *day bed with back support*

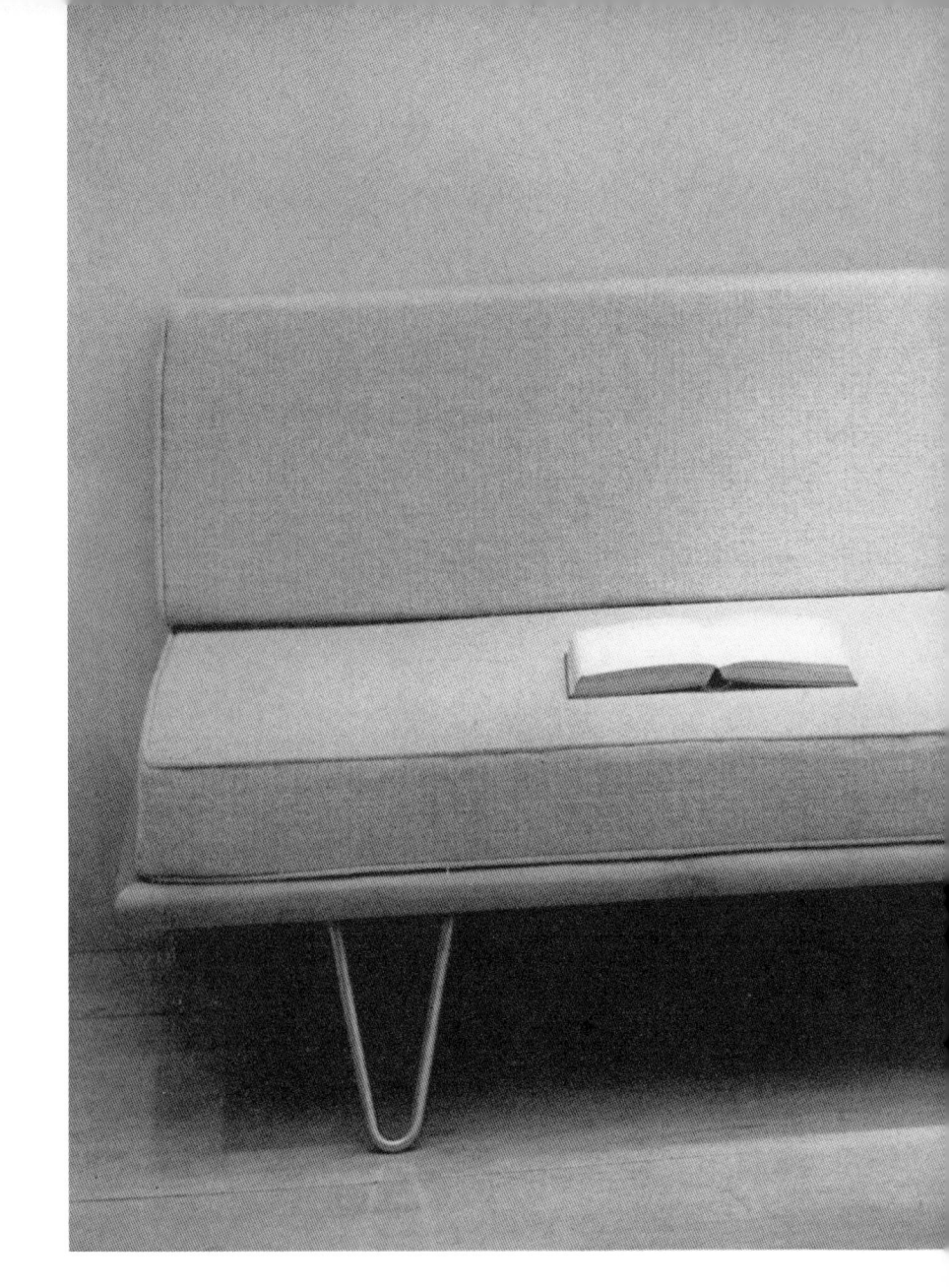

5087 *day beds,* 652 *corner unit,* 4950 *tray table*

4681 *(29" wide)*

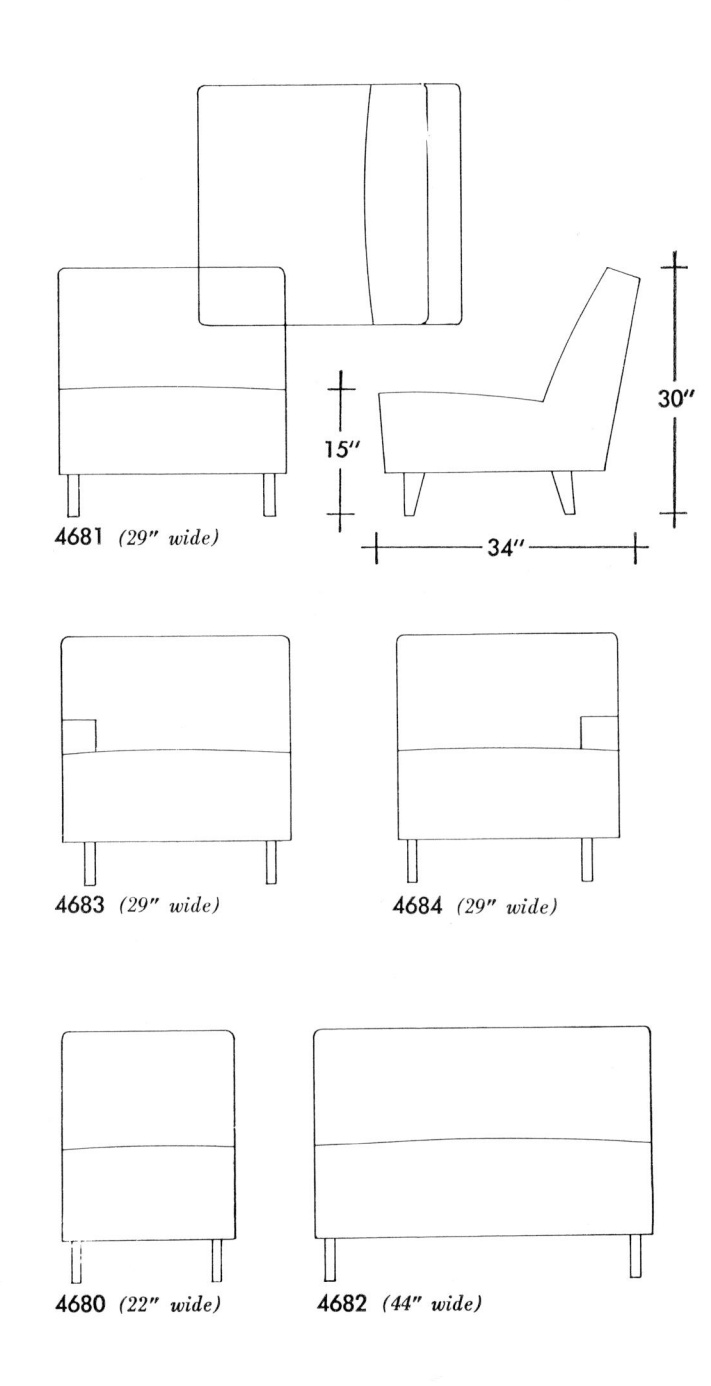

15" 30" 34"

4683 *(29" wide)*   **4684** *(29" wide)*

4680 *(22" wide)*   **4682** *(44" wide)*

4683   4680

56

652 *corner unit*	4681	4682	4634-L *lamp table*	

The sectional seating pieces (above) are constructed of foam rubber and springs, with birch legs finished natural or to match any of the other standard wood finishes. Accessory pieces include corner and chairside units (see p. 68), lamp tables, end tables and tray table (see pp. 64-65). Matching ottoman, armchair and sofas are shown on following page.

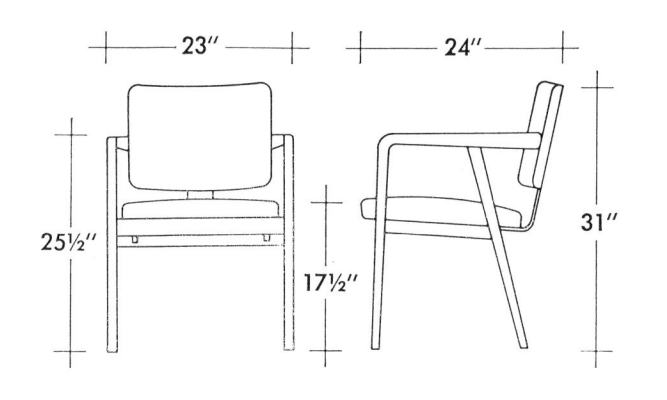

4663 Light upholstered armchair, foam rubber and springs. Birch frame may be finished natural or to match any of the other standard wood finishes.

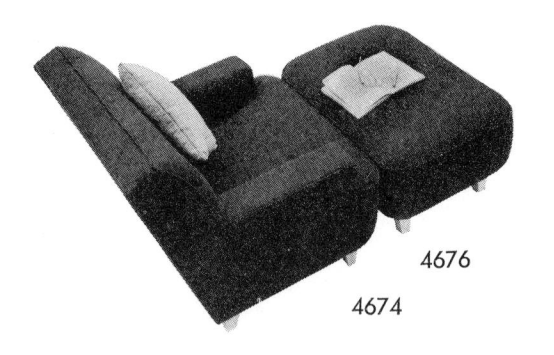

4676
4674
4678 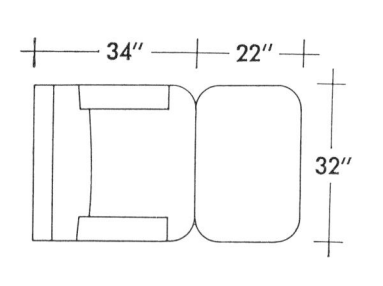 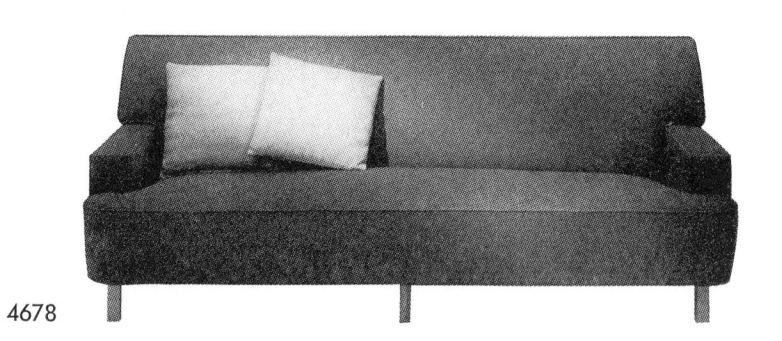

The easy chair, ottoman and sofas (above and right) form a coordinated group together with the sectional seating units shown on preceding spread. Foam rubber and springs, legs birch finished natural or to match other standard wood finishes. 4677 (two-seater) 64" wide, 4678 (three-seater) 80" wide.

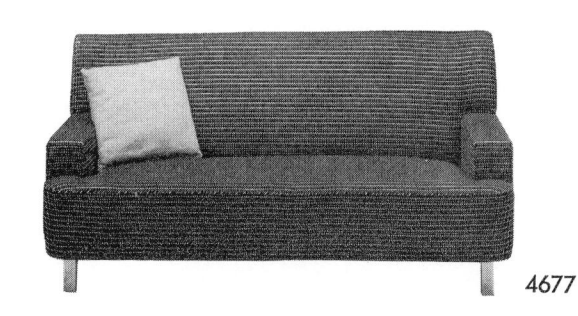

4677

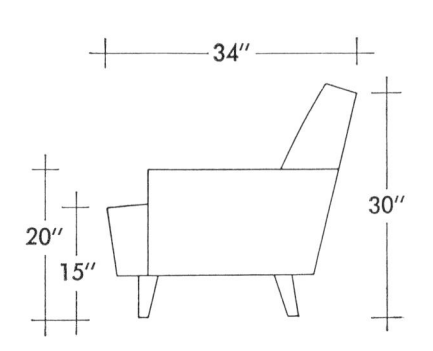

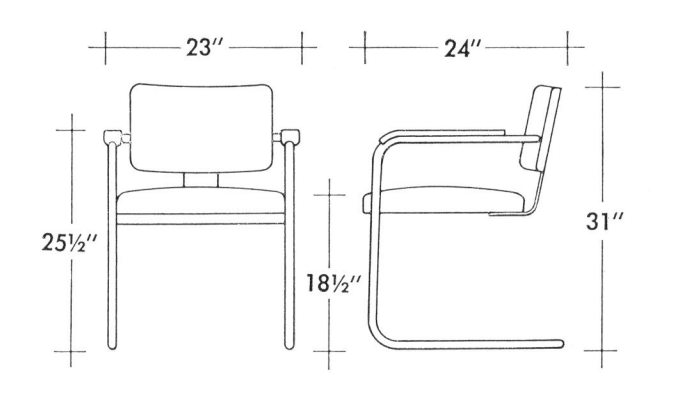

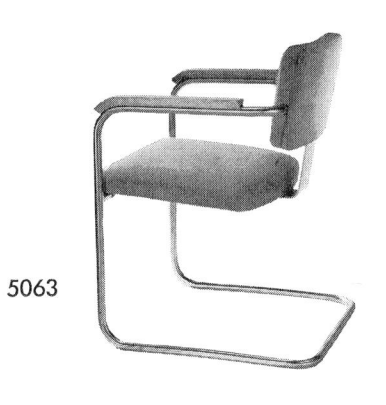

5063 Light upholstered armchair, foam rubber and springs. Tubular frame brushed chrome; birch armrests finished natural or to match other standard wood finishes.

4688 / 4774 Easy chair with loose cushion (left), foam rubber and springs; W: 27", D: 30", H: 32". Open-arm lounge chair (right), foam rubber and springs; birch frame finished natural or to match any of the other standard wood finishes; W: 26½", D: 32¾", H: 29¼".

5080 Open-arm easy chair, foam rubber and springs; metal angle frame in dull white or black enamel; birch armrests may be finished natural or to match any of the other standard wood finishes.

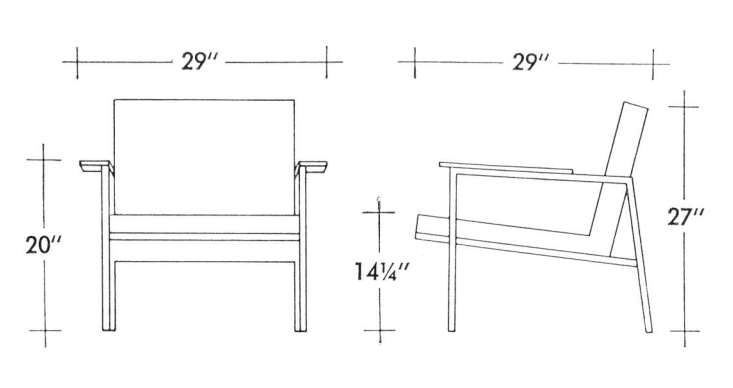

6152 6252

The Hansen group, designed by Hvidt-Nielsen and manufactured in Denmark, is a small collection of seating units and tables, all built in a combination of solid and laminated wood. From the viewpoint of craftsmanship all of the pieces are remarkable. The table legs, for instance, are designed with a unique spread top of laminated wood, and they attach to the top members with the rigidity that comes only with high-precision workmanship.

Tables include round and rectangular side

6102 *side chair*
6002 *arm chair*

6852
6952
6862

6352

6052

6972
6573

tables in two heights. The conference table shown directly above is 24 inches high (at least five inches lower than standard tables of this type) and introduces a new note of ease and informality when used with low armchairs. The chairs, illustrated at the extreme right and left, are built in plywood and padded leather or fabric. The latter (right) is particularly serviceable, for the seat and back can be removed for cleaning or replacement without recourse to the upholsterer's tools.

6802
6812

6062 *arm chair*

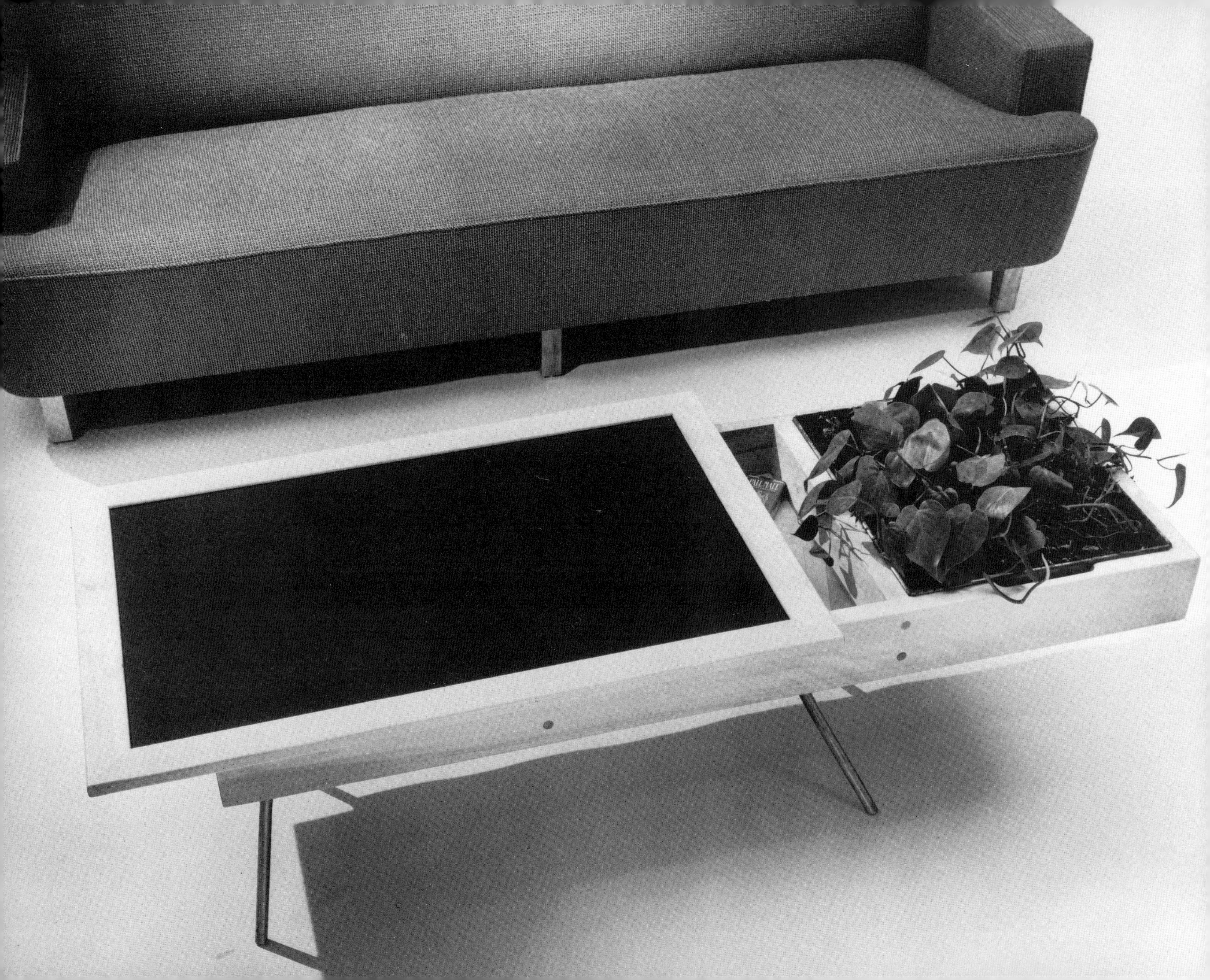

4652

4652 coffee table (above) may be extended to six feet by pulling out the two racks concealed in its ends. Each rack contains a removable serving tray with white hard plastic bottom (top right), and rim finished to match table. Should the extension feature be desired without serving, the trays can be reversed (lower right) as their undersides are also finished to match the table. All standard wood finishes; legs usually ebonized or matching. H: 18", Top: 24" x 36" (closed).

4662 coffee table with insert for plants (facing page). Top is surfaced with hard plastic (choice of five colors) and slides back to reveal a storage compartment for cigarettes, matches, ashtrays, etc. Left end of the table is open and large enough to hold a dozen magazines. Birch finished natural or to match any of the other standard wood finishes; satin aluminum legs. H: 16", Top: 22¼" x 50".

4662 *coffee table*

5058 coffee table with plant insert; top surfaced with hard plastic (choice of five colors), birch rim and legs finished natural or to match standard wood finishes. H: 15", Top: 40" dia. 5059, same without plant insert.

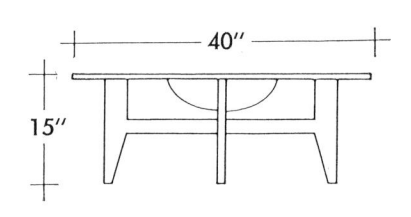

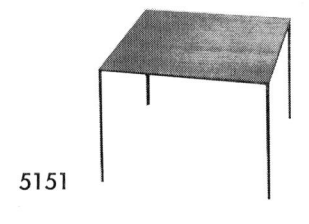

Square table (left), 34" x 34", 22" high, and oblong coffee table (right), 17" x 48", 16" high, are available with plain or textured hard plastic tops; metal angle frames in dull white or black enamel.

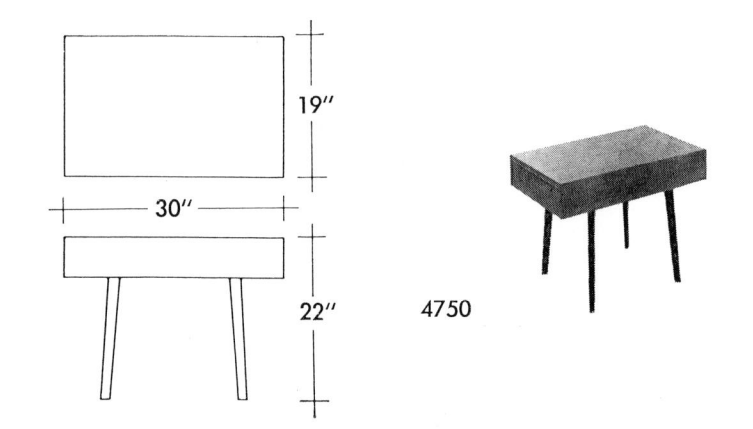

4750 end table with drawer (left). All standard wood finishes; top covered with genuine leather, legs usually ebonized or matching table.
4744 chairside table (right) with glass top, drawer, plant boxes and additional magazine space in rear. All standard wood finishes, 5½" legs; lines up with corner unit (p. 68); 17 13/16" x 34", 22 5/16" overall high.
4745, same without plant boxes. 4745-L, same as 4745 with built-in lamp as used for 4634-L.

64

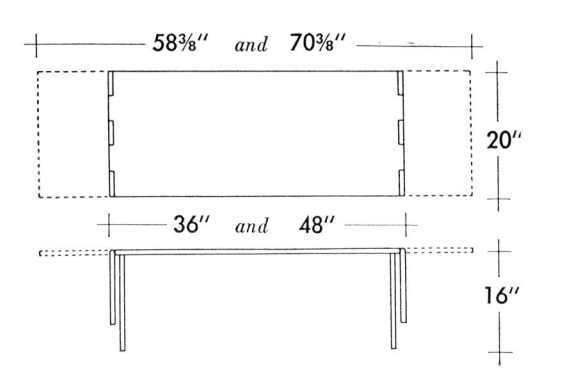

Drop-leaf coffee table, available in two sizes: 20″ x 48″, closed (5057) and 20″ x 36″, closed (5055). All standard wood finishes, brushed chrome legs.

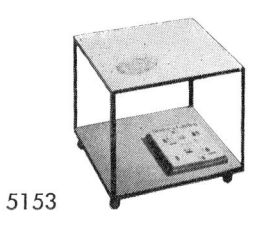

Mobile table (left), 24″ x 24″, 20″ high, and oblong mobile table (right), 17″ x 24″, 24½″ high, are available with plain or textured hard plastic tops; metal frames on casters in dull white or black enamel.

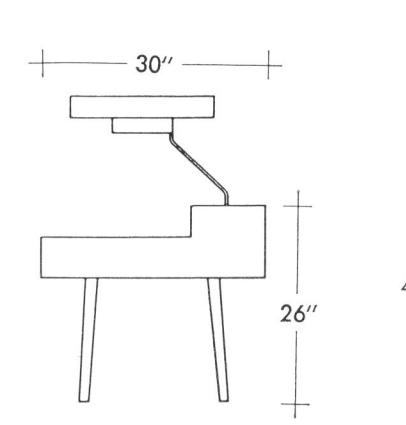

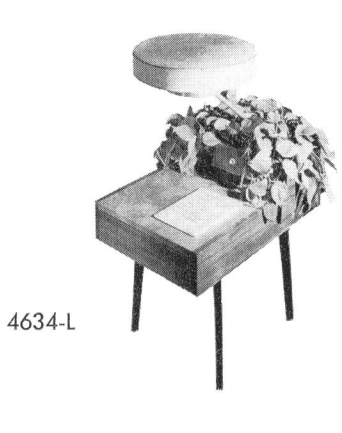

4634-L lamp table (left), equipped with plant boxes, drawer and built-in circline fluorescent lamp with translucent shade on satin aluminum swivel stem. All standard wood finishes; legs usually ebonized or matching table. Top: 19″ wide, covered with genuine leather.
4634, same without built-in lamp.
4950 molded plywood tray table, 15″ x 15″; extends from 19″ to 33″ in height, walnut or calico ash with polished chrome support (right).

65

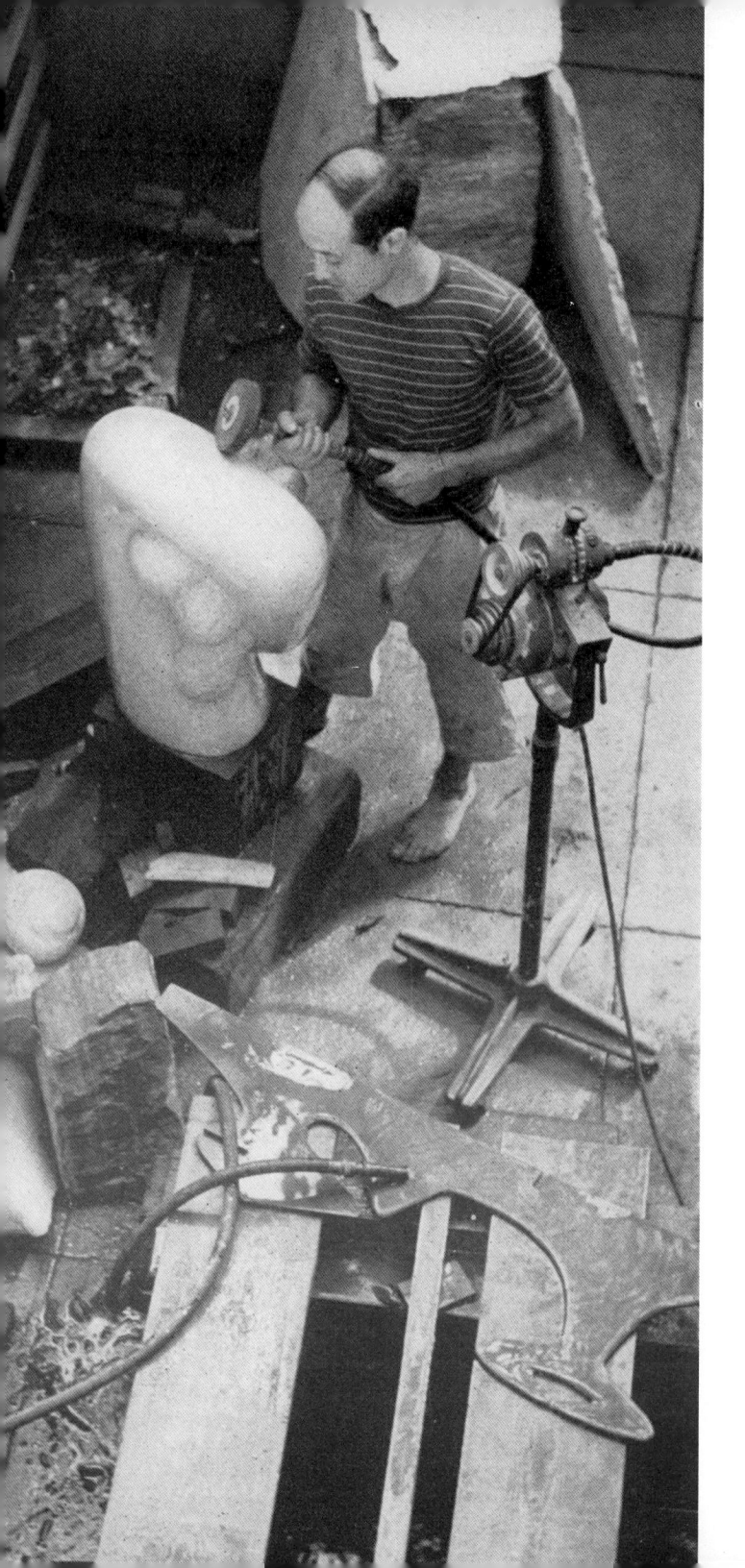

Isamu Noguchi is one of America's most distinguished sculptors. Born in Los Angeles in 1904, he lived in Japan from the age of two until he was thirteen, in Indiana until he was seventeen, in New York for the next four years and then in Paris. Background for this life on three continents was a well-known Japanese poet for a father and a Scottish mother. It was Noguchi's original intention to be a doctor, but on his return from Paris, where he studied with Brancusi, he exhibited as an abstract sculptor. After a short period of working as a portrait sculptor, he went to China and Japan, later on lived in England, and for the past dozen years has spent most of his time in New York. Unlike most sculptors, Noguchi has shown an extraordinary range of interests: he designed the Radio Nurse, has done all of Martha Graham's sets since 1942, has designed playground equipment, toys and lighting units. The remarkable thing about this phase of Noguchi's activity is that while his designs are always brilliantly conceived in relation to the production process to be used, he always works as a sculptor, imparting to the most inconspicuous objects a thoroughly personal feeling. It should be added that while this activity represents a very substantial body of work, he has executed an impressive number of sculpture commissions, including the large overdoor panel for the Associated Press Building in New York, a 70-foot colored cement wall sculpture in Mexico, and, more recently, the controversial sculpture panels for the SS Argentina. Noguchi's furniture in the Herman Miller collection shows the same characteristics as his other designs for industry — magnificently proportioned shapes, logically designed for production.

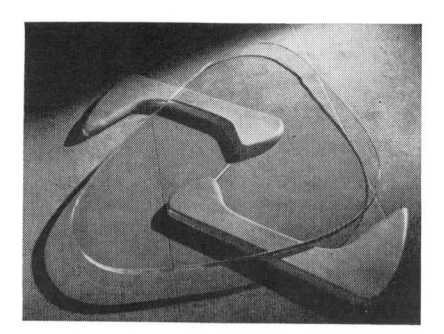

IN-50 coffee table, 36" x 50", 15" high; tawny walnut on solid walnut, natural or ebonized on solid birch.

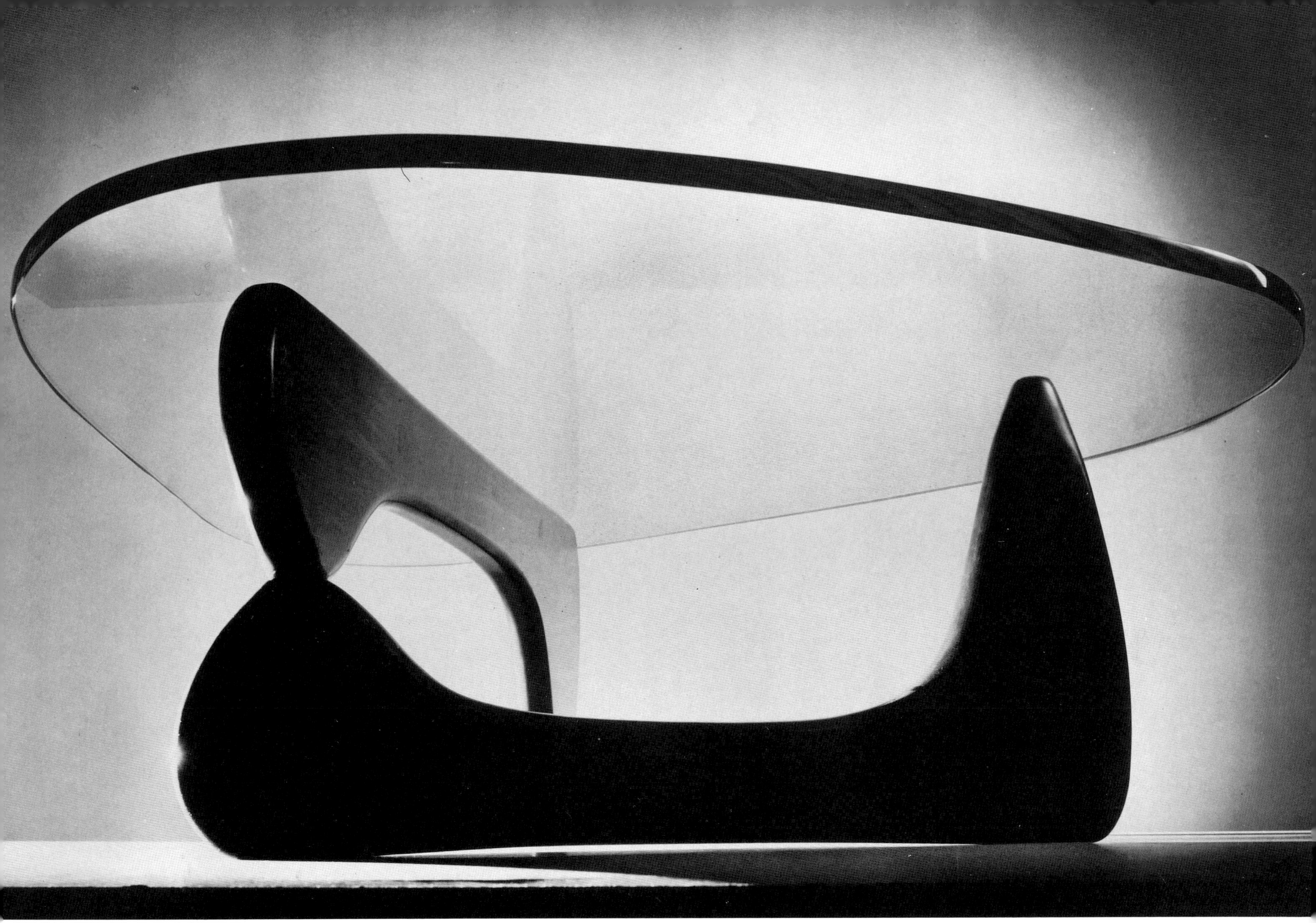

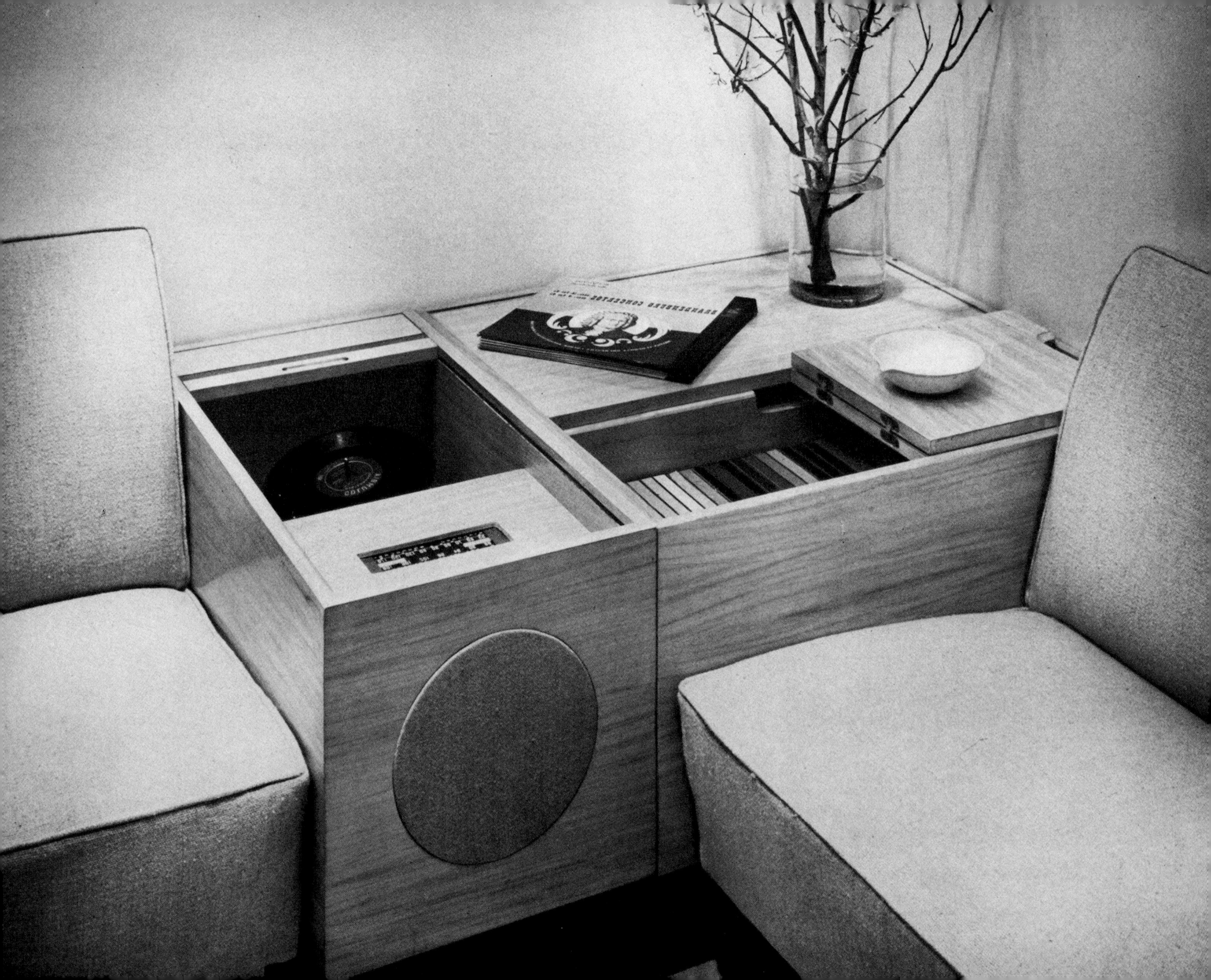

4742 *chairside unit* 17⅛" w. x 34" d. x 22 5/16" h.
652 *corner unit* 34" w. x 34" d. x 22 5/16" h.

4625-A

4663

4613-TV

4741

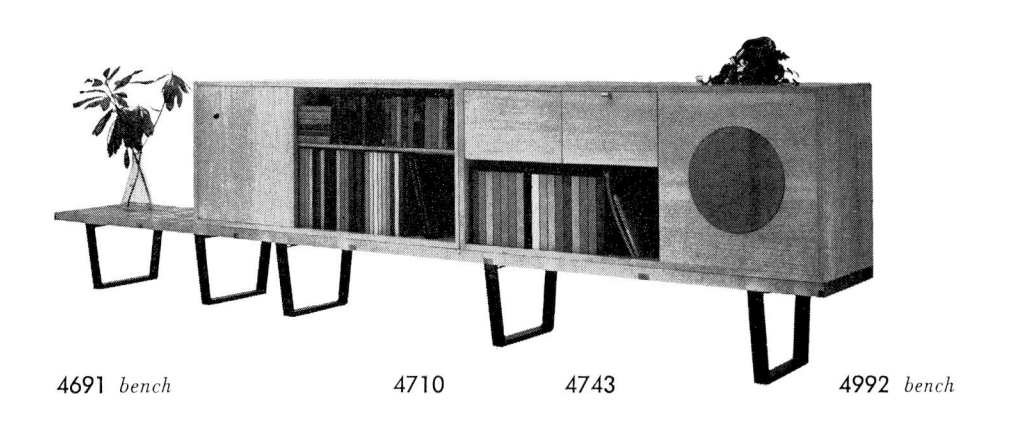

4691 *bench*   4710   4743   4992 *bench*

Cabinets for installation of phonograph, radio, speaker and television are available in various modular sizes, as indicated in diagrams on pp. 16-19. They may be combined with matching units for book and record storage, in groups of 34" high cases on 5½" legs (above) or 24" high cases on 14" platform benches. The phonograph-radio-record storage combination (facing page) serves in a corner arrangement of the seating units shown on pp. 56-58. 652 corner unit, 34" x 34", 22 5/16" over-all high; storage space for records, blankets, etc., below removable hinged top sections. 4742 chairside phonograph-radio unit with tambour top, 17⅛" x 34", 22 5/16" over-all high; purchaser to make necessary cut-outs in blanks and install his own equipment; cloth-covered opening for 12" speaker is provided. 5142, same without speaker opening, for use with remote speaker. All Standard wood finishes, 5½" legs; top sections of 652 corner unit may also be finished in any of the standard lacquer colors. Other units for use with 652 are shown on p. 64.

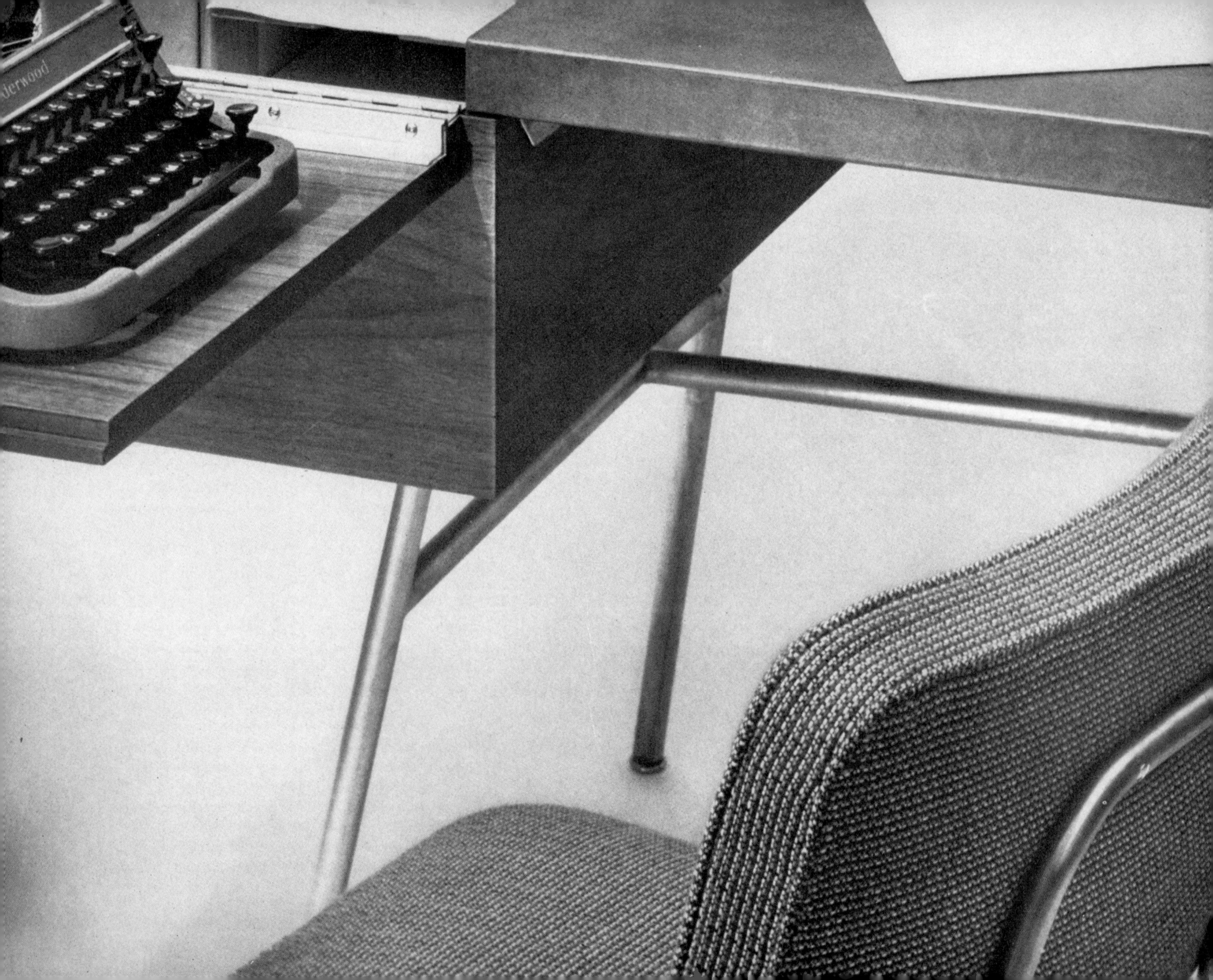

work 1

While the contemporary residential interior has been demonstrating a steady evolution towards a more "workmanlike" kind of space — easier to furnish and take care of — the executive office has been going through an equally interesting development towards the warmth and informality of the well-appointed home living room. It has become more and more common, for instance, to find that the conference area in executive offices is not the desk, but a coffee table flanked by sofas and comfortable chairs. Because of the overlapping nature of the design trends in home and office it seemed appropriate to expand the Herman Miller Collection to include furniture for both types of interiors. The work units illustrated in this section are unique in their flexibility, efficiency and luxurious craftsmanship.

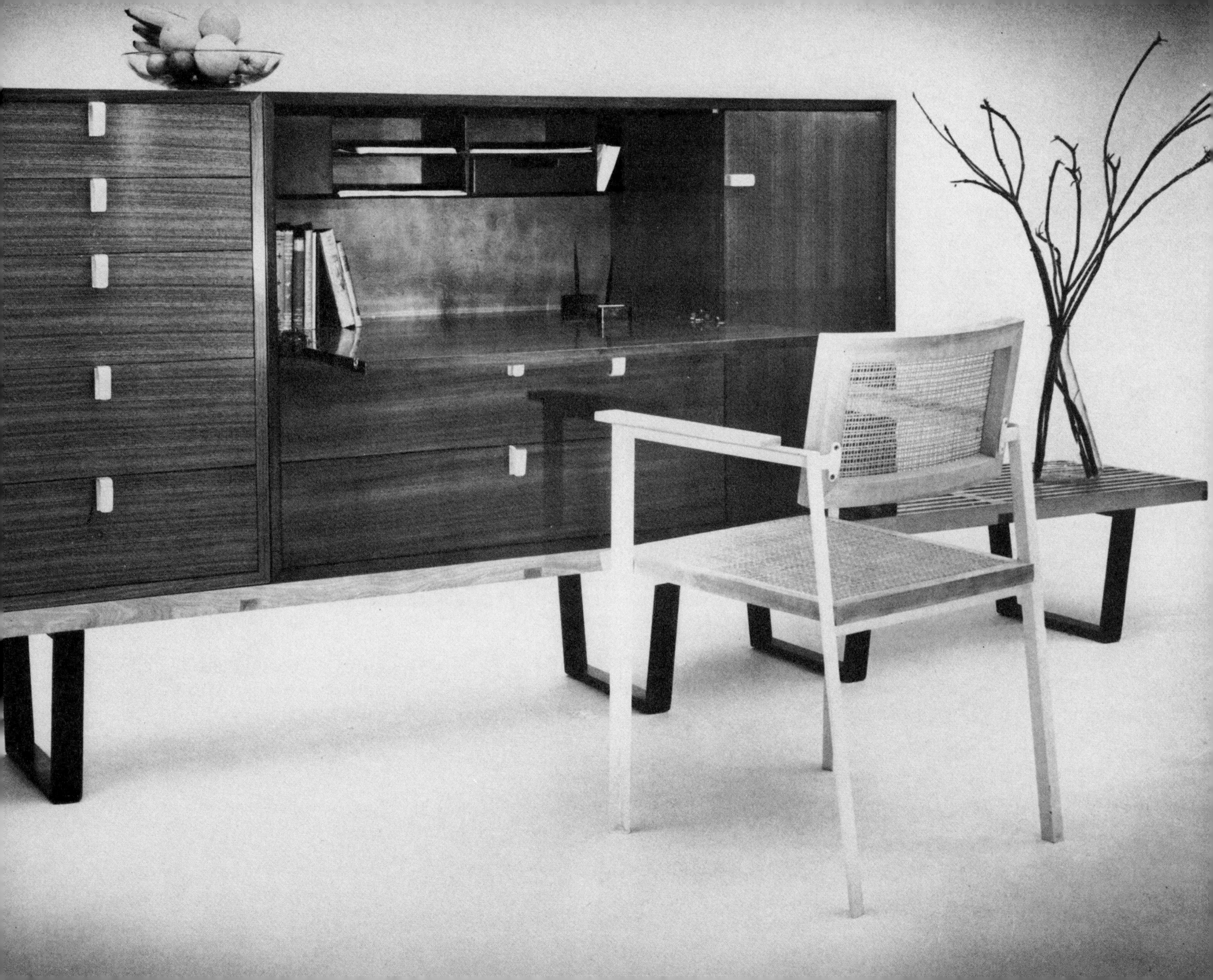

4610
4931
5069 *chair*

4622

4623

4741

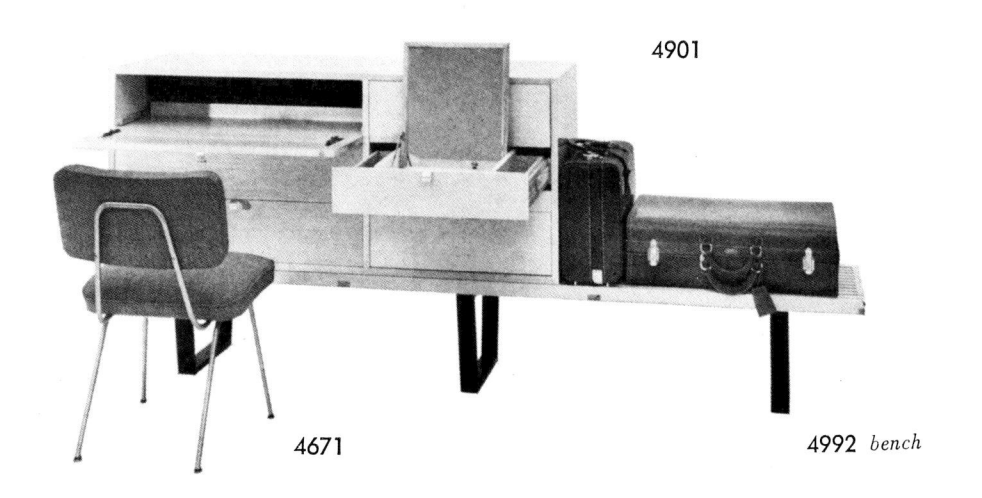

4901

4671

4992 *bench*

A variety of chest desks in 24″ and 34″ heights may be lined up with matching storage units or radio-phonograph-television cabinets on 5½″ legs or 14″ platform benches, as indicated in diagrams on pp. 16-19. All drop-leaf desks are furnished with pigeonhole units (ebonized) and some may be ordered with built-in fluorescent desk lights. 4623 (above) and 4901 (left) have drop-leaf pull-out desks; the latter is used as a guestroom unit since it also contains a vanity drawer on extension slides. 4931 (facing page) is part of a series of 34″ high chest desks for use on 14″ high platform benches, combining maximum desk space with ample storage facilities (see pp. 18-19).

4658

This desk presents one of the most difficult problems encountered by the furniture designer. If he follows the traditional solution of two three-drawer pedestals flanking a knee space and a center drawer, he ends up with a collection of seven nondescript drawers and a generally cramped space for legs and knees. If he re-studies the whole problem, he arrives at a design whose appearance baffles the conventional-minded. In an effort to develop a really workable home desk, Herman Miller produced the unit illustrated on these pages, and its wide acceptance indicates that there is a sizable public which will approve of unfamiliar forms if greater utility is achieved. The desk consists of a container for a portable typewriter on the left; a top covered with genuine leather or plastic fabric, and a working height extension slide file basket including a Pendaflex file at the right. Above the desk there is a storage unit whose contents are instantly located. Storage for typewriter materials—paper, carbon, ribbon, etc.—is located in the typewriter compartment itself. The entire desk is supported by a cradle of tubular steel, finished in a satin chrome. For those who want more in a desk than undifferentiated storage space, whose requirements call for a fine working instrument, this unit is recommended. All standard wood finishes. Top 28″ x 54″, 28″ high. Over-all height including top unit: 41¾″.

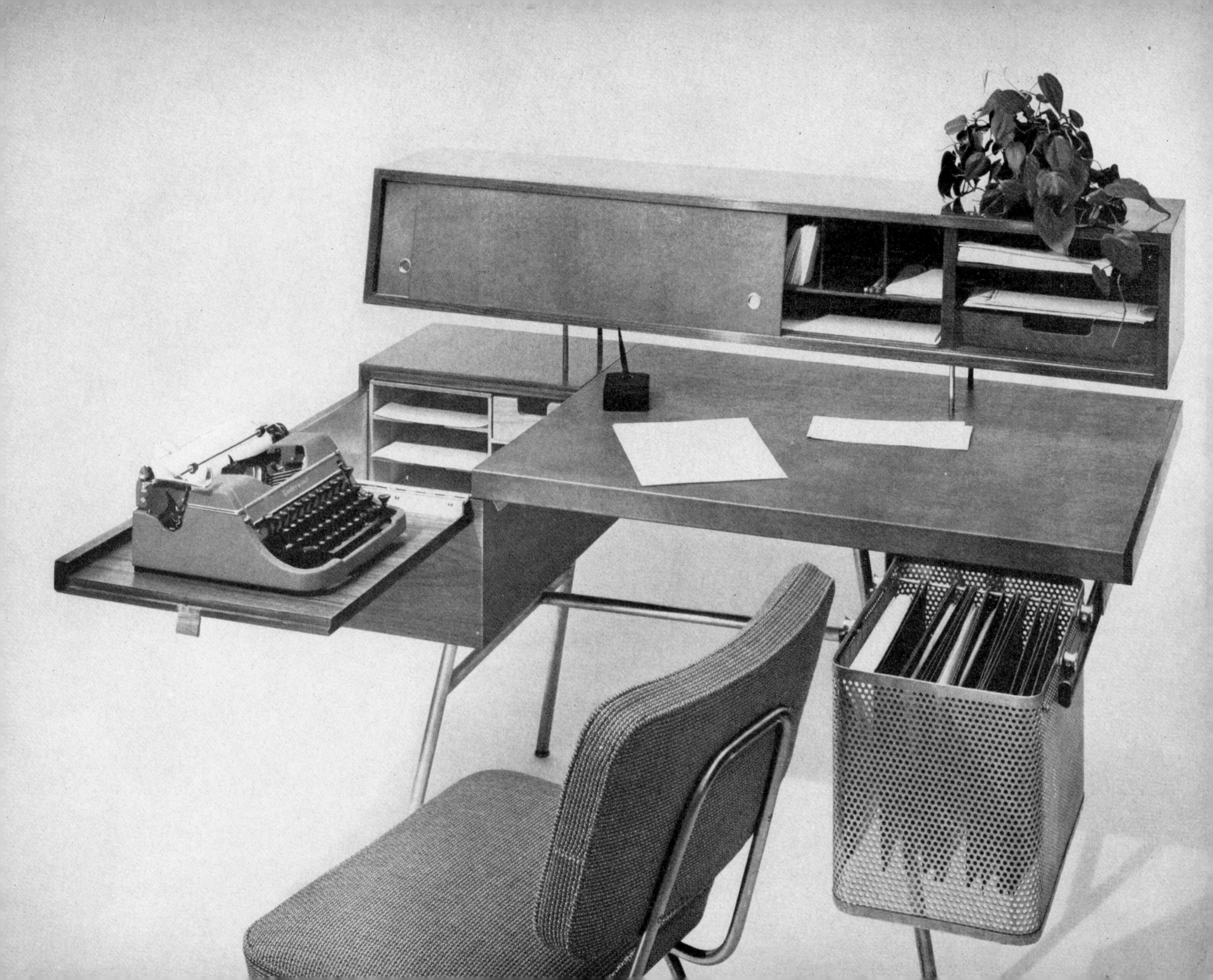

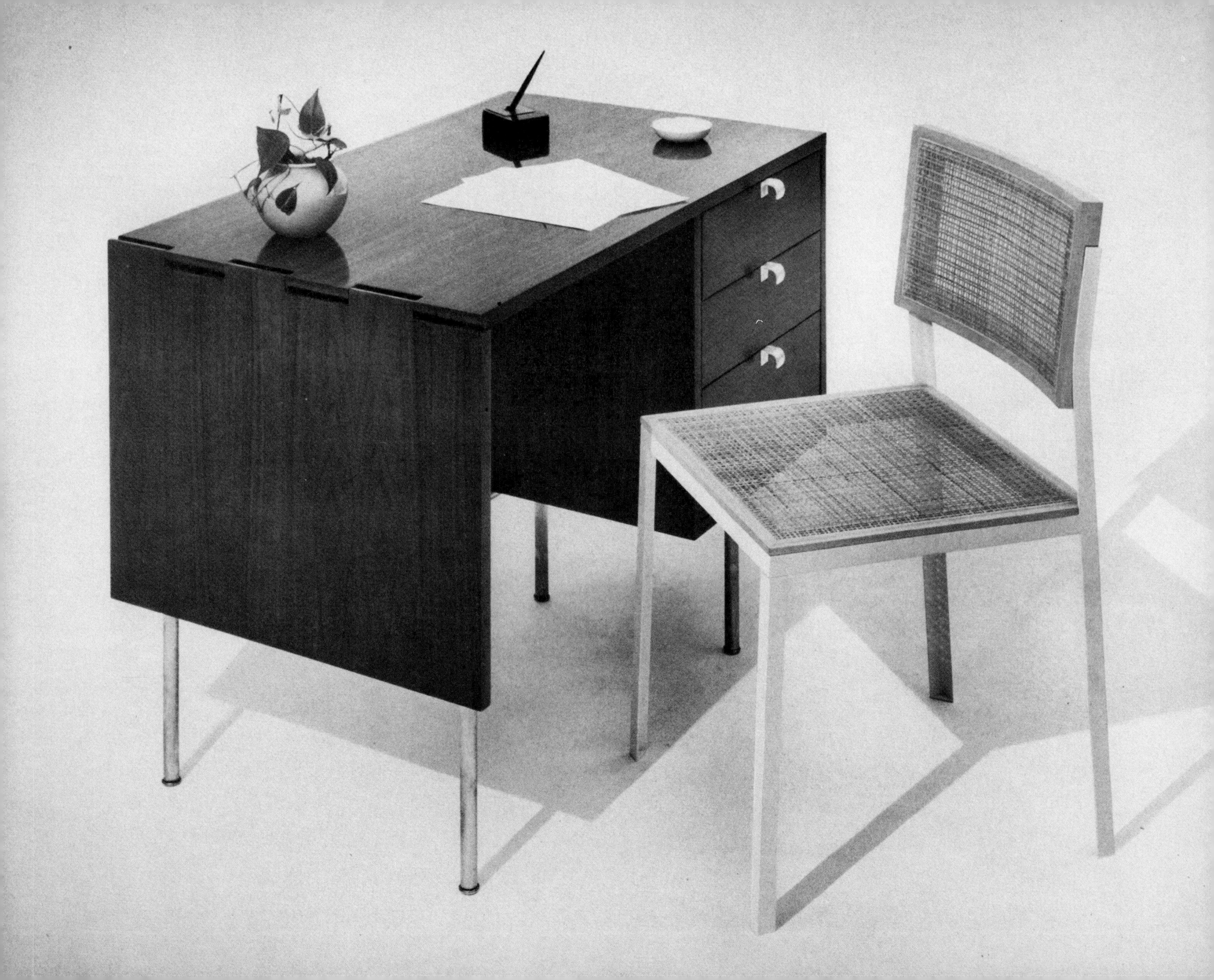

4754 *desk*
    24" w. x 40" l. x 29½" h. (closed)
    24" w. x 58-3/16" l. x 29½" h. (open)
5068 *side chair*

4752 *typing unit*

4663 *chair*

8430-X *table*

4754 drop leaf desk (facing page). All standard wood finishes, satin chrome legs. 4753 reversed. 4752 typing unit (above) contains four drawers, extension-slide file basket at working height and a hanger for typewriter case. All standard wood finishes, satin chrome legs. 4751 reversed. Also available without file basket. 8430-X table (above). Top; standard wood finishes or hard plastic (choice of five colors). Base brushed chrome, dull black or white enamel.

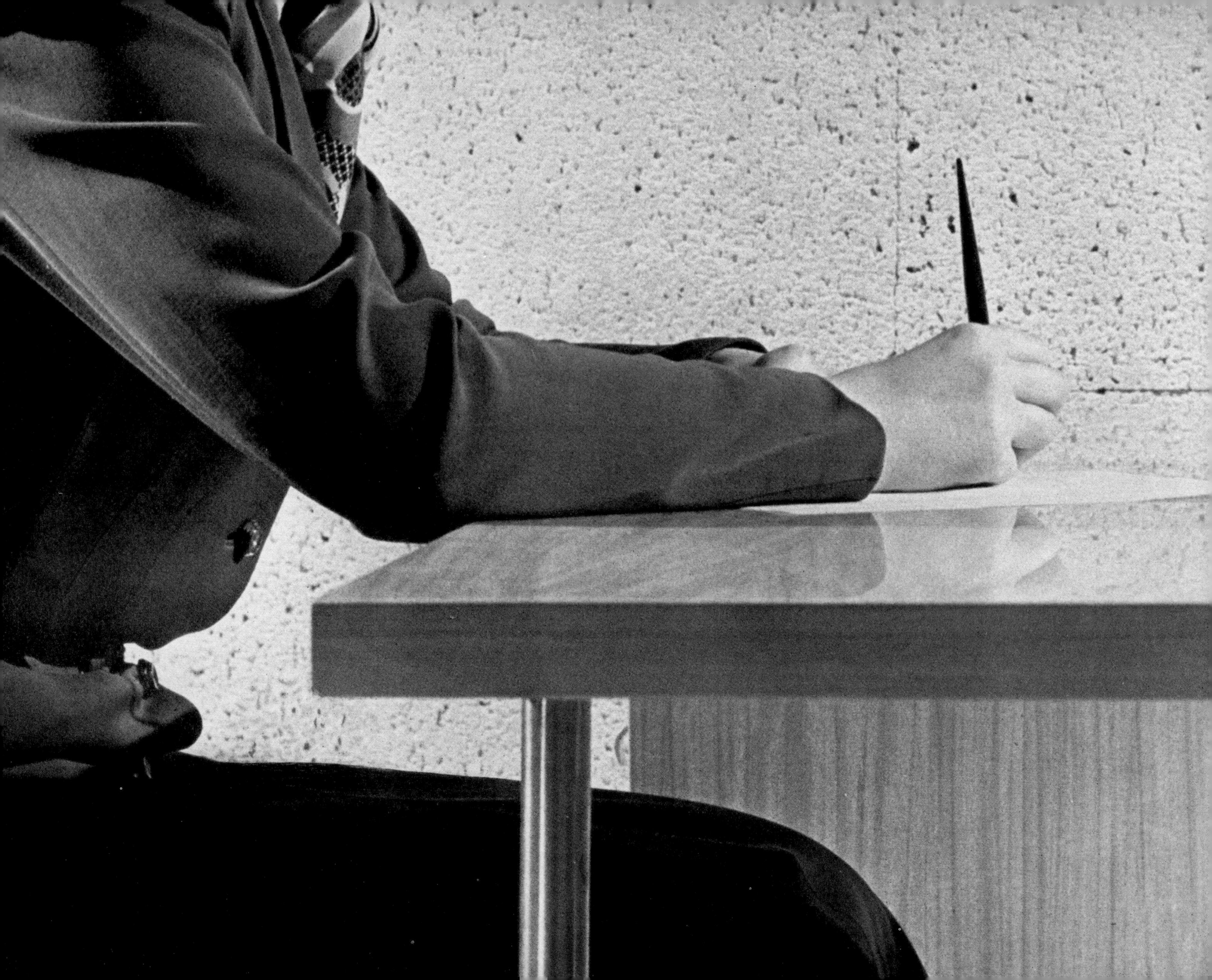

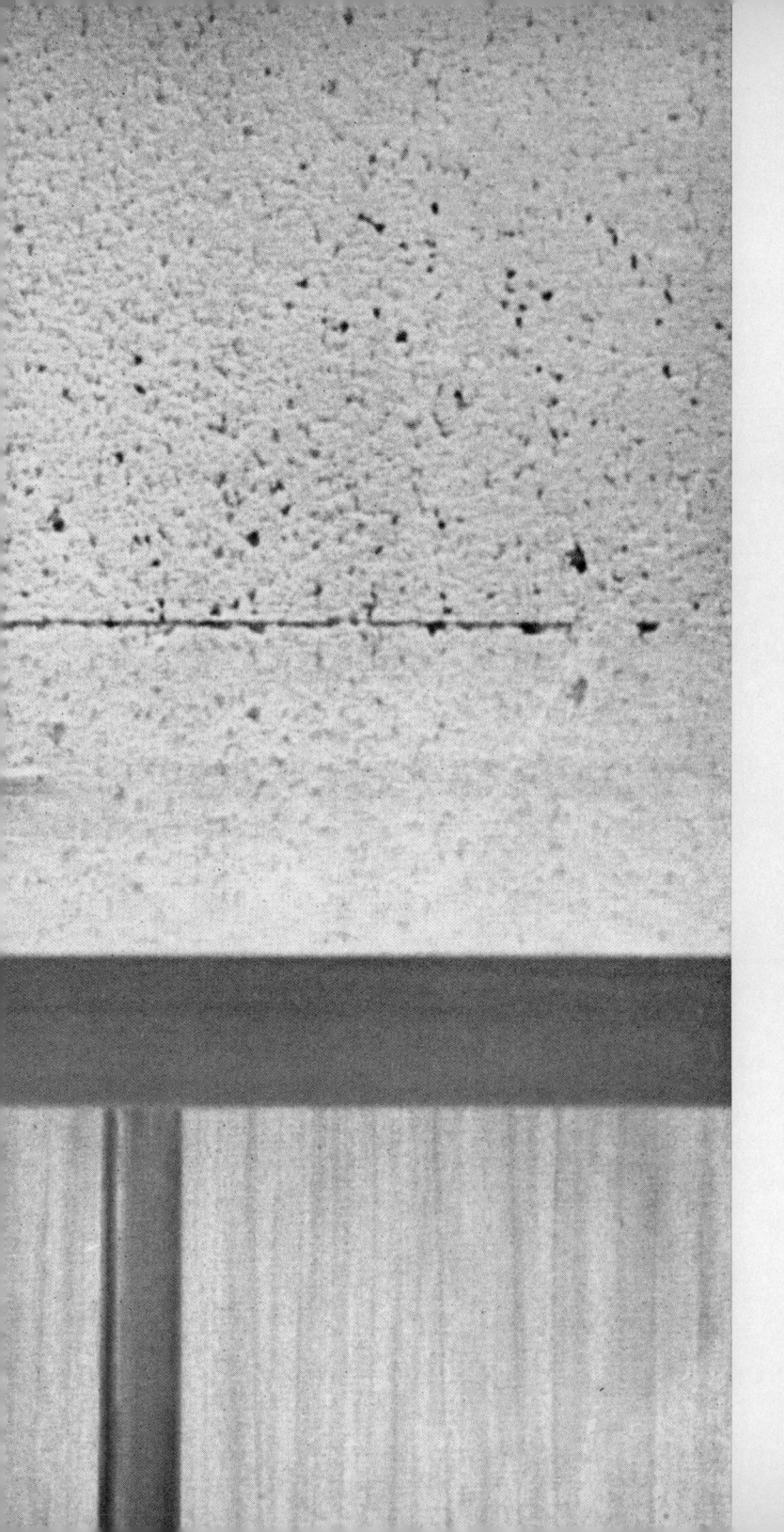

work 2

Although statistics made by home economists show with unfailing regularity that most families use the home as a place for study and office work, the need for appropriate work surfaces and storage is not always recognized. In its provisions for this kind of activity the Herman Miller Collection is unique, as the pieces shown in this section cover almost every situation. For apartments and small homes there are several composite units, suitable for living or bedrooms, which contain drop-leaf desks along with other storage facilities. The home desk (page 74) is a complete "workshop" with built-in provisions for a portable typewriter, visible storage, and desk-height file basket. A drop-leaf desk (page 76) folds into a very compact piece, while the typing unit (page 77) instantly converts any table into a reasonable approximation of the best office furniture.

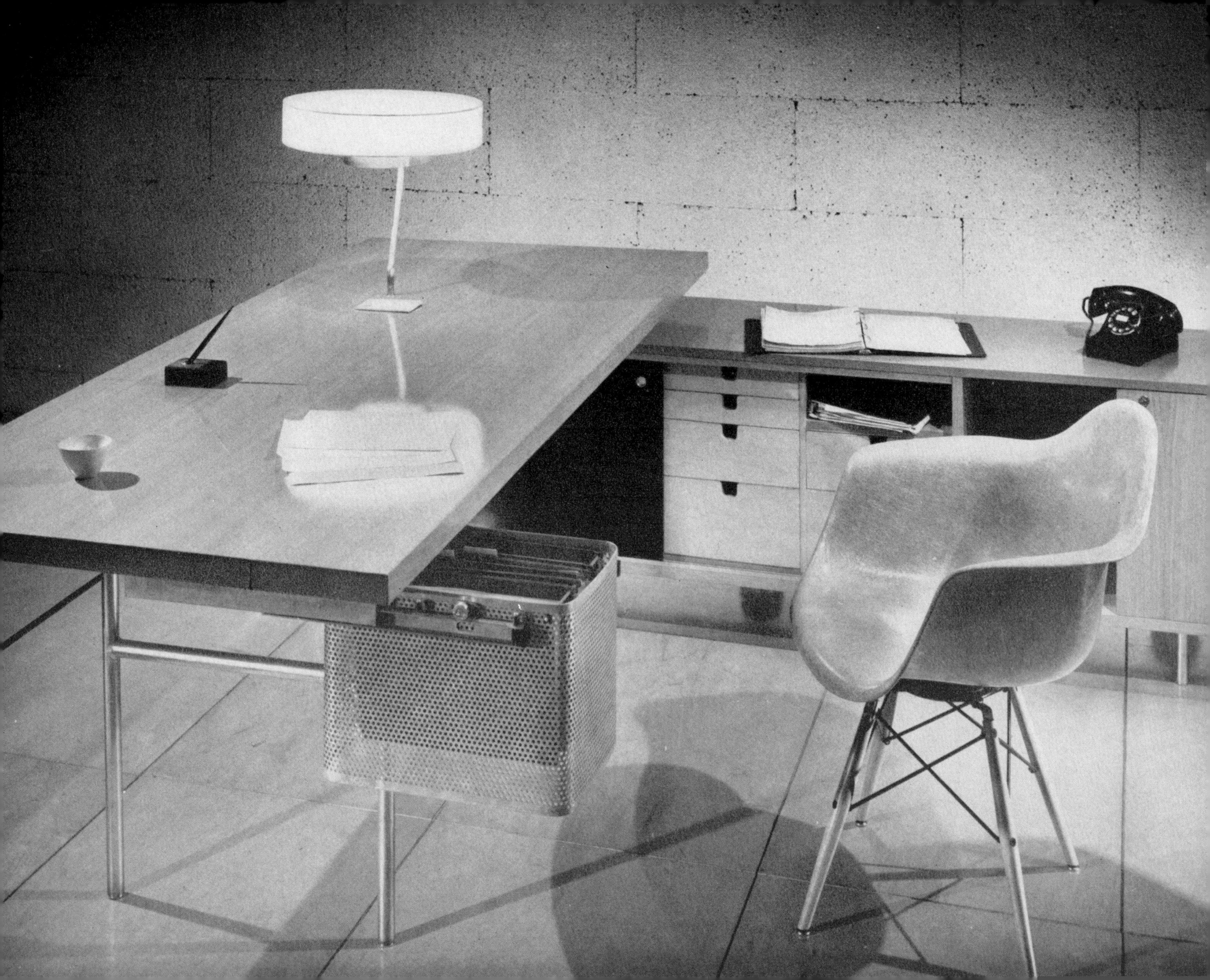

EOG—The Executive Office Group by Herman Miller—is designed to meet the requirements of modern architects, interior designers and office planners. Designed by the office of George Nelson, an organization which works in the fields of architecture and interior design as well as furniture, EOG is the result of years of study, research and the actual testing of ideas in daily practice.

The EOG design approach offers these many advantages to the modern planner: 1—it eliminates the bulky traditional knee-hole desk, replacing it with a free-floating work surface, 2—it eliminates the need for scattered storage pieces around the room, concentrating the facilities in a unit whose contents are visible and accessible from the desk chair, 3—it makes available important accessories (built-in lamp, desk-height file) formerly provided only in custom furniture, 4—it frees the rest of the office space for the kind of informal seating being used more and more for discussion and conference.

The trend in office design today is towards an interior which functions more efficiently—but more unobtrusively—than its predecessors. The contemporary executive office is a daytime living room where work can be done under less tension with fewer distractions. It was to make possible this most modern of working interiors that the Executive Office Group was developed.

Left: A typical EOG installation. Executive desk with 7230-L top, PB-1 file basket, CL-1 lamp, 8010 storage unit and PAW-swivel chair.

Above: Executive desk with 7230-R top, SC-72 screen and 8011 storage unit. Note compartment with sliding door in rear of storage unit.

Executive desk with 7230-L top, PM-3 drawer unit, 8010 storage unit and 4663 chair. For variations see diagrams on facing page.

Standard finishes. DESK TOPS: Tawny Walnut (TW), Comb Grain Oak (CGO), Chili Walnut (CW), Ebonized (E), and Hard Plastic (choice of white, light grey, mustard, buff and turquoise).

STORAGE UNITS: Shell and hinged door—Tawny Walnut (TW), Comb Grain Oak (CGO), Chili Walnut (CW), or Ebonized (E). Sliding doors—Bittersweet Red (R), Forest Green (FG), or Gunmetal (GM). Drawer unit PM-3 always matches shell of storage unit. Trays (inside)—Natural Birch (B).

The basic executive desk consists of a slab supported at one end by a metal leg unit; at the other end by one of several storage components. In its simplest form the desk is adequate for most requirements. It can be furnished with a variety of accessories and also with various combinations of storage as shown at the right.

Where a more solid appearance is considered desirable, it is recommended that the cane screen illustrated above be used. Where the L-unit is selected, the entire arrangement should be kept clear of the wall since there is storage space available in the rear of the storage unit. In ordering this, "L-arrangement" should be specified.

Another frequently used combination is illustrated below and is particularly suitable where space is somewhat restricted or where the desk is to be treated as a relatively inconspicuous part of the interior design. For use in this arrangement specify desk top as "wall-hung" and storage unit as "separate."

6720, *as shown* (6721, *reversed*)

8010, *as shown* (8011, *reversed*)

6722, *as shown* (6723, *reversed*)

8014, *as shown* (8015, *reversed*)

CI-1

PB-1

PM-3

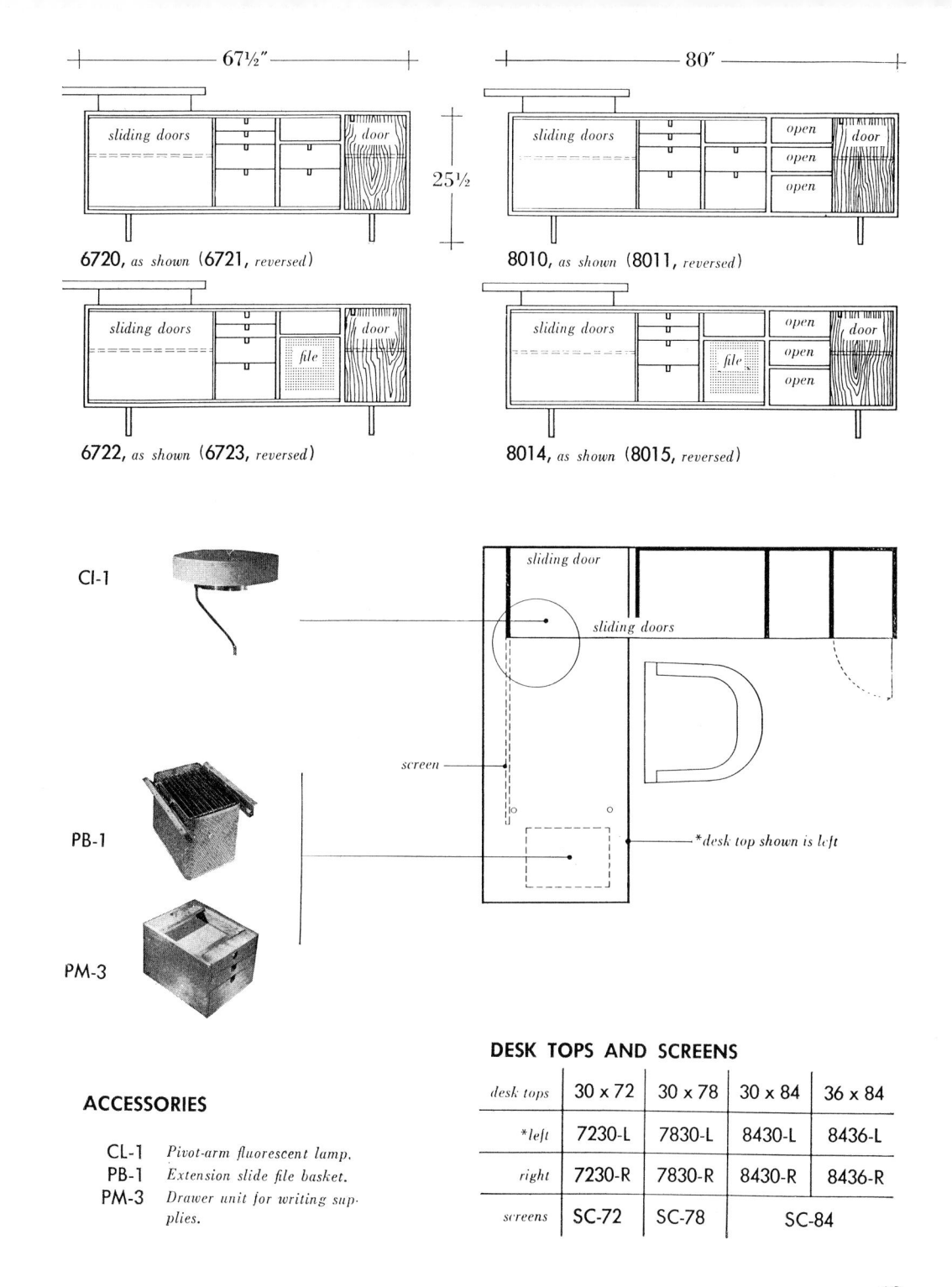

ACCESSORIES

CL-1   *Pivot-arm fluorescent lamp.*
PB-1   *Extension slide file basket.*
PM-3   *Drawer unit for writing supplies.*

DESK TOPS AND SCREENS

desk tops	30 x 72	30 x 78	30 x 84	36 x 84
*left	7230-L	7830-L	8430-L	8436-L
right	7230-R	7830-R	8430-R	8436-R
screens	SC-72	SC-78	SC-84	

8033, as shown (**8032**, reversed) — 80" × 25½"

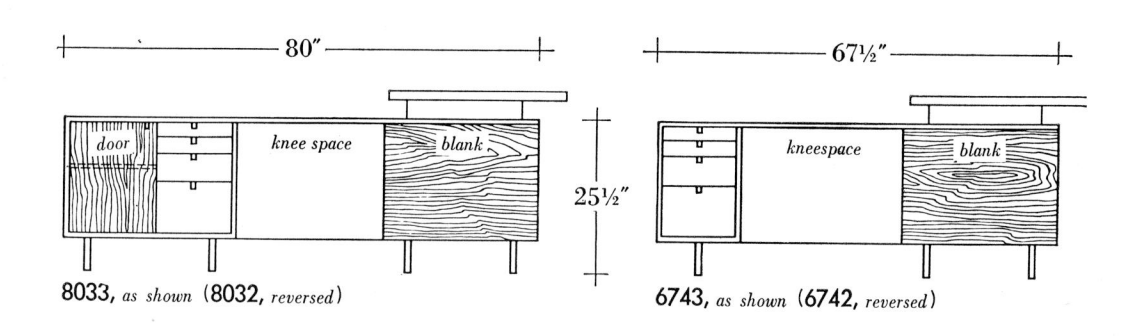

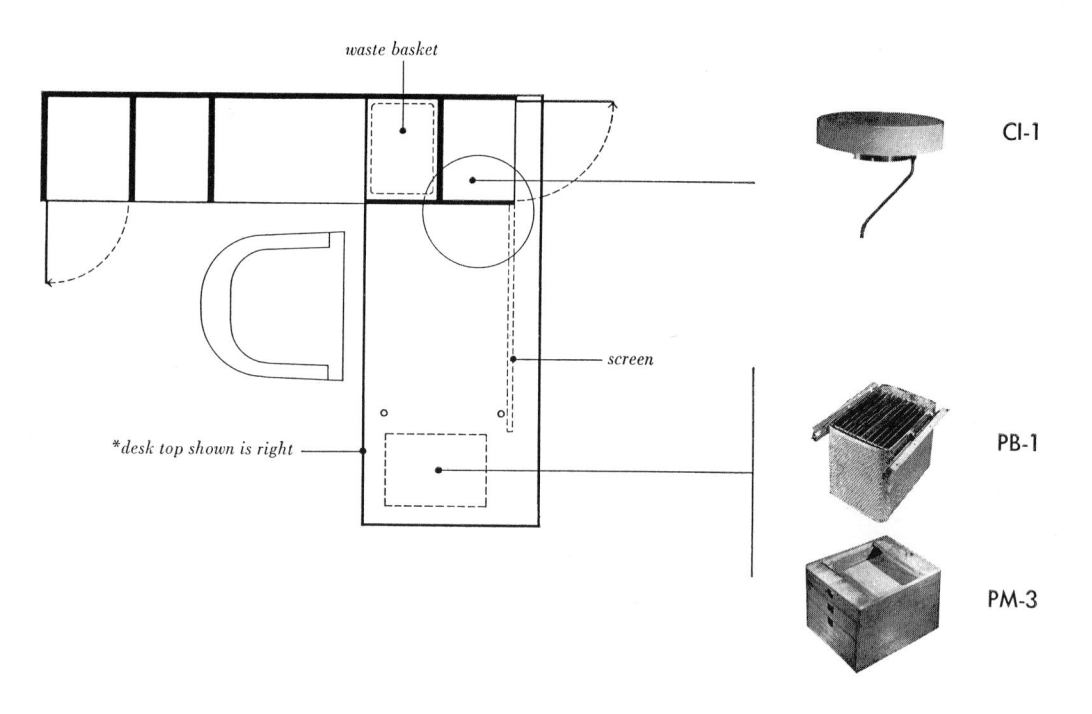

6743, as shown (**6742**, reversed) — 67½"

desk top shown is right

CI-1
PB-1
PM-3

DESK TOPS AND SCREENS

desk tops	30 x 72	30 x 78	30 x 84	36 x 84
left	7230-L	7830-L	8430-L	8436-L
*right	7230-R	7830-R	8430-R	8436-R
screens	SC-72	SC-78	SC-84	

ACCESSORIES

CL-1   *Pivot-arm fluorescent lamp.*
PB-1   *Extension slide file basket.*
PM-3   *Drawer unit for writing supplies.*

The work center for the executive secretary is generous with respect to both size and equipment. The typewriter has its convenient permanent location adjoining the desk. The larger of the two storage units contains not only drawers of adequate capacity, but a cabinet for personal belongings and supplies. Two basic arrangements of this unit are possible — the L-type, shown above and on the facing page, and the parallel, illustrated directly below. Accessories available include the built-in lamp, desk-height file basket and extra drawer unit.

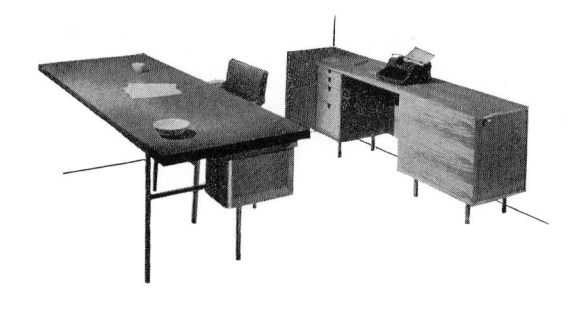

Secretarial desk with 7230-R top, PB-1 file basket, CL-1 lamp, 8033 storage unit and 4663 chair. For variations see diagrams on facing page.

Standard finishes. DESK TOPS: Tawny Walnut (TW), Comb Grain Oak (CGO), Chili Walnut (CW), Ebonized (E), and Hard Plastic (choice of white, light grey, mustard, buff and turquoise).

STORAGE UNITS: Shell and door—Tawny Walnut (TW), Comb Grain Oak (CGO), Chili Walnut (CW), or Ebonized (E). Drawers—Natural Birch (B).

6030D-L, *as shown* (**6030D-R**, *reversed*)

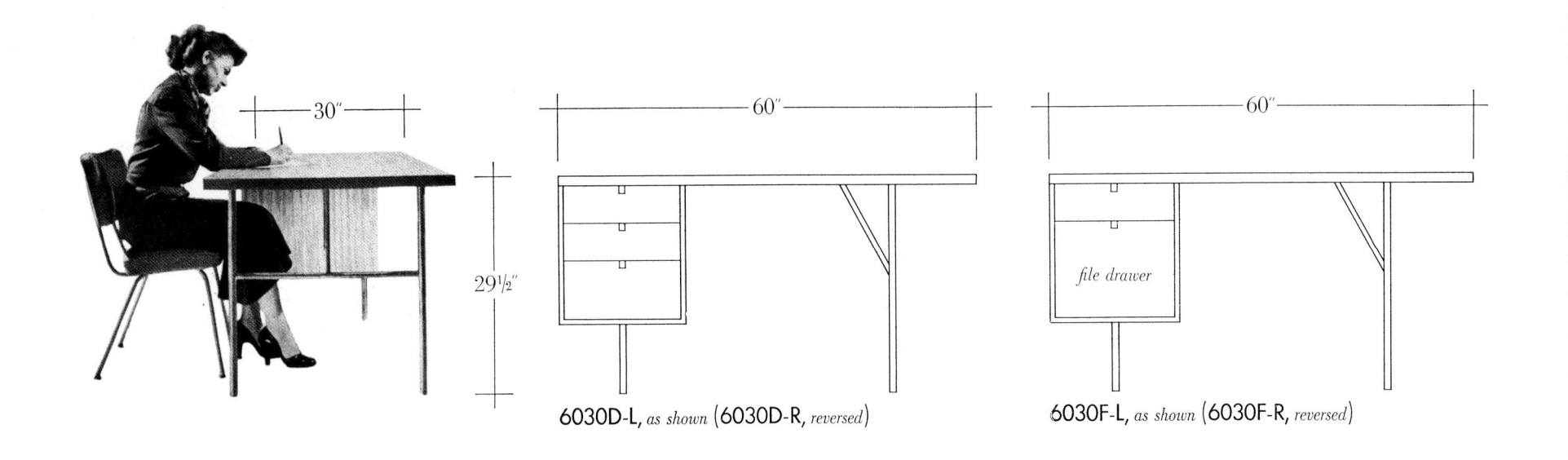

6030F-L, *as shown* (**6030F-R**, *reversed*)

The small desk shown on these two pages was designed to meet a variety of requirements. It may be used in groups in an office where the furniture is to harmonize with the larger pieces in the executive offices. As an occasional desk requiring a minimum of space it is particularly useful because the storage compartment set high off the floor and the metal legs eliminate the usual appearance of excessive bulk. The storage compartment comes in two versions: a three-drawer unit and a file-plus-drawer unit.

A variety of accessories may be used with the small desk, notably the special typing table (right), complete with four drawers and a file basket, and an over-desk tray, TU-1 (see facing page) for papers and correspondence.

Though conceived essentially for office use, this desk will prove a boon to many a busy housewife or to the executive accustomed to doing some of his work at home.

4751
4752 *reversed*

A typical office arrangement using 6030F-L desk with TU-1 over-desk tray, 4751 typing unit and 4663 chairs.

Standard finishes. Tawny Walnut (W), Comb Grain Oak (CGO), Chili Walnut (CW), or Ebonized (E). Desk tops can also be furnished in Hard Plastic (choice of white, light grey, mustard, buff and turquoise).

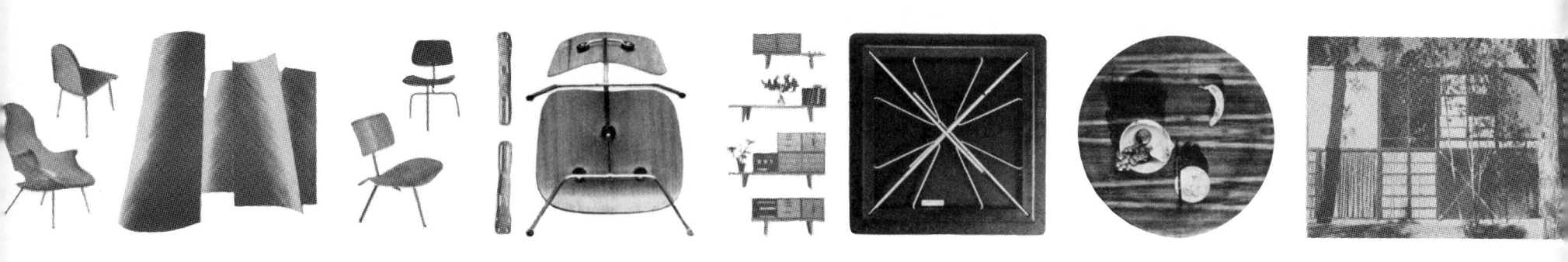

Those familiar with the Eames designs shown in the first edition of this book will readily grasp, in going through these pages, the extraordinary development during the past three or four years. To the original molded plywood group have been added the now-familiar plastic chair, a remarkably flexible series of storage units and the new upholstered wire chair. While very different from each other in technique and appearance, all illustrate a uniquely imaginative and realistic approach to materials and processes, and they exemplify without exception Eames' constant preoccupation with the idea of service—the dedication of design to the creation of improved performance at reduced cost. Charles Eames came into furniture design as an architect and it is as an architect that he still works today. His own house, a brilliant and sensitive use of standard steel building components, is as well known to professionals the world over as his furniture. The most recent project in architecture brings to the problem of the under-$10,000 house the same depth of perception and clarity of thinking which has so delighted the users of his seating and storage pieces. It is also as a contemporary architect in the most contemporary sense that Eames disregards the boundary lines which have traditionally divided his profession from other areas of creative activity. "The Toy," which received nation wide attention last year, is as consistent with his outlook as his buildings and furniture, and there is now in existence a brilliant series of experimental films — not yet shown to the public — which represent a new expression of his continuing interest in problems of form, color and movement. Also in preparation is a color film for Herman Miller showing the development and production of the molded plywood, plastic and wire chairs.

Nothing could illustrate more clearly the relationship between the company and its designers than the fact that the movie was half completed before Herman Miller executives learned that a film was being made for them — or than when the news was received their only reaction was to set up a budget for its completion.

production die for plastic shell ⇒

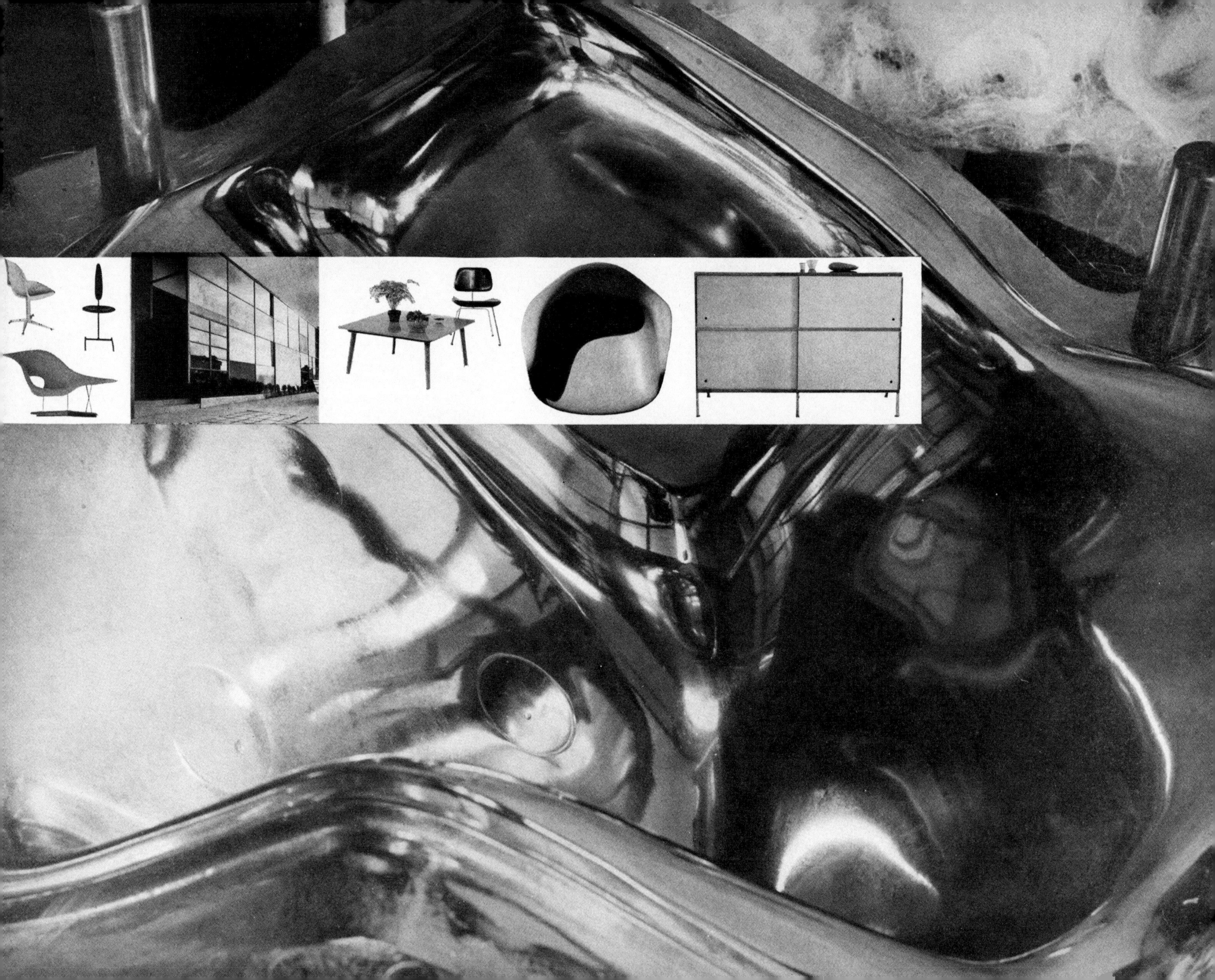

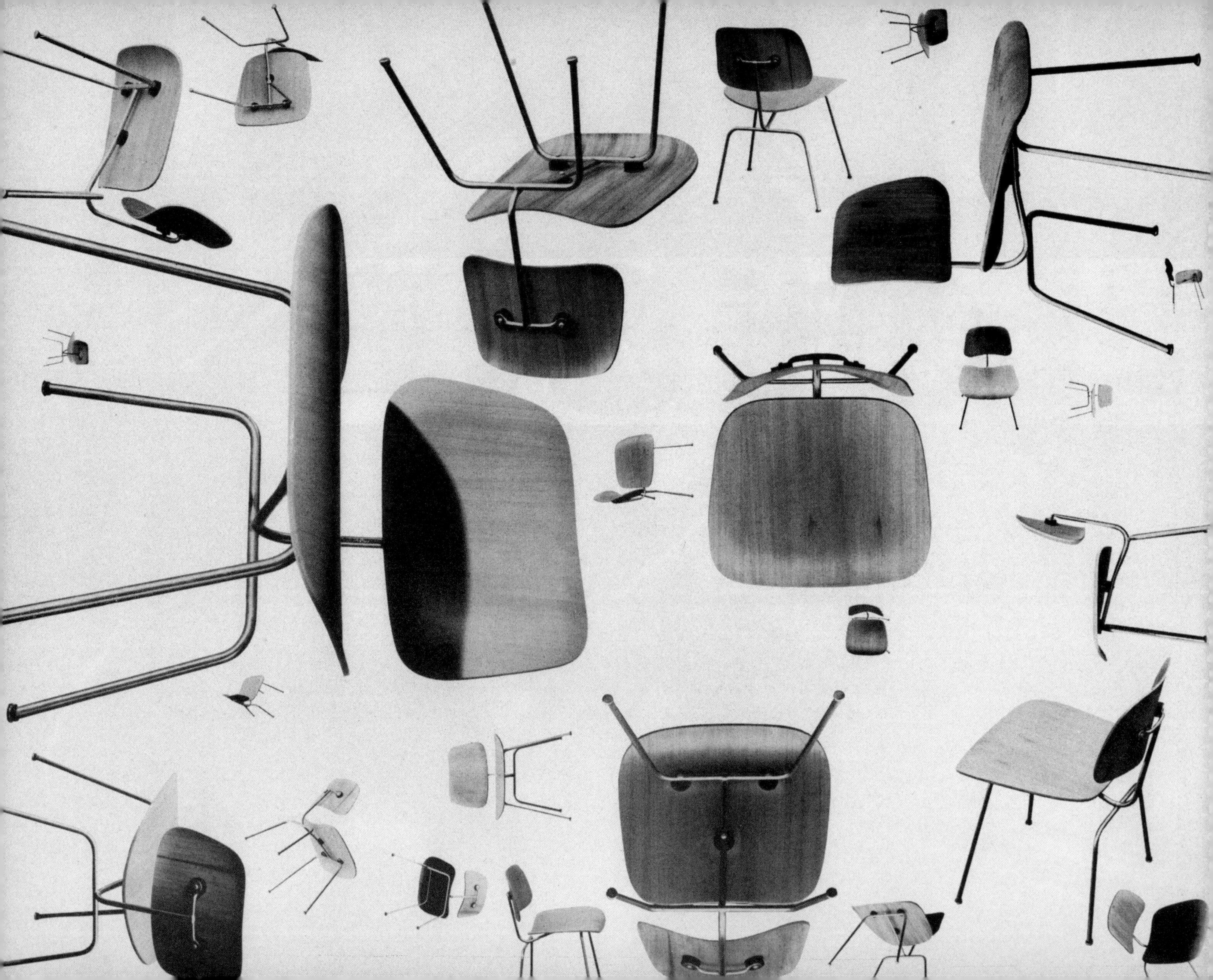

molded plywood chairs

THE EAMES MOLDED PLYWOOD CHAIR has become a classic. Its clean details and sculptured curves have shown what beauty can come from modern production techniques. The seat and back, molded to the contours of the human body, together with the rubber mounts which permit the chair to flex with any shifting of position, provide comfort rarely found in a non-upholstered chair. The chair is now available in two basic models, a dining chair and a lounge chair, each available with wood or metal legs; also with fabric, leather or calfskin upholstery over a layer of foam rubber. All covers are permanently applied to the plywood.

WOOD FINISHES Birch
Walnut
Calico Ash
Black
Red
Oak

METAL FINISHES Chrome
Black

weights shown are net uncrated
scale silhouettes shown on a 2" grid

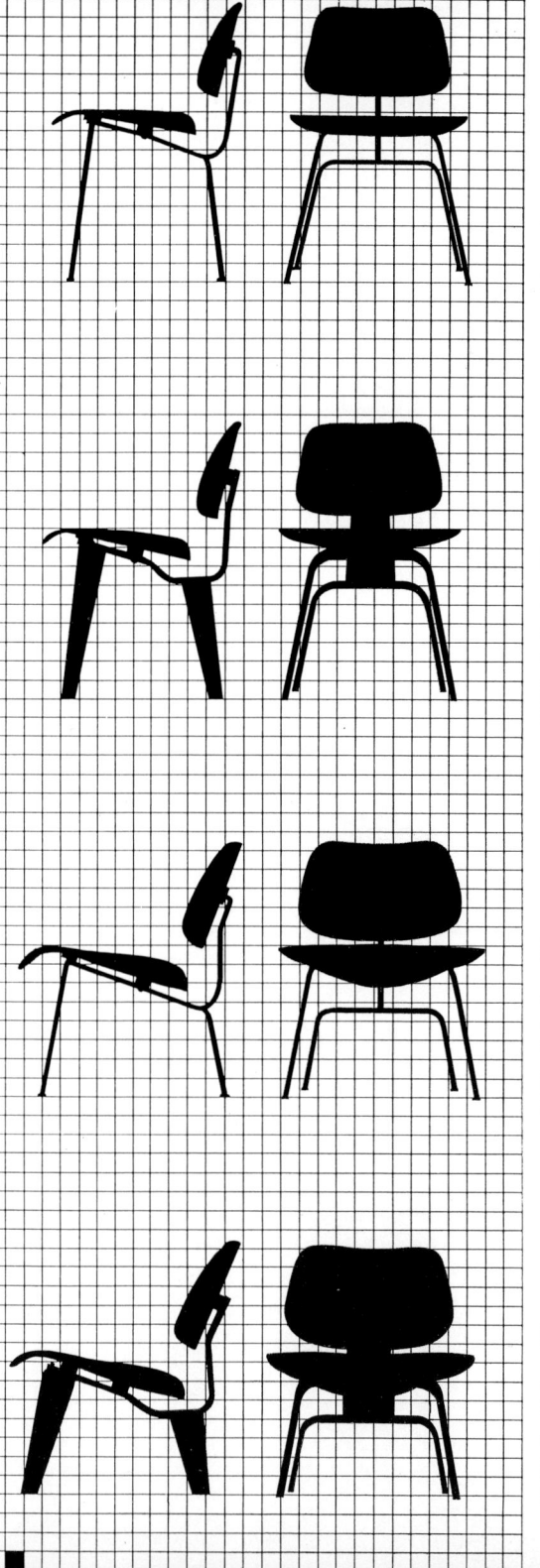

DCM
Dining chair—metal legs. Seat 18" high. Also an excellent desk chair.

HT.	W.	D.	SEAT HT.	WT.
29¼"	19½"	21¼"	18"	15 lb.

DCW
Dining chair—wood legs. Seat height 17½". Also suitable as a desk chair.

HT.	W.	D.	SEAT HT.	WT.
29⅞"	19½"	21¼"	17½"	10 lb.

LCM
Lounge chair—metal legs. Angle and height of seat suitable for reading, conversation and lounging.

HT.	W.	D.	SEAT HT.	WT.
27⅜"	22¼"	25⅜"	15¼"	14 lb.

LCW
Lounge chair—wood legs. Similar in design and proportions to LCM. An ideal chair for relaxation.

HT.	W.	D.	SEAT HT.	WT.
27⅜"	22¼"	25⅜"	15¼"	10 lb.

IT DTW-3 DCM DCM DCW DCM

LCW CTM LCM LCM

molded plastic chairs

THE PLASTIC SHELLS of these armchairs are molded of a thermosetting resin reinforced with glass fibers. (In aircraft production this combination of materials is used where high resistance to impact and weather is mandatory.) The metal bases are made of rod or wire, finished in bright zinc (a plated finish) or black oxide (a durable, chip-resistant finish). Both of these finishes are mar and weather resistant. The wood legs of the DAW models are of natural walnut or birch, the rockers of the RAR model of natural birch.

The inherent properties of the materials used in this chair make it a thoroughly practical piece for many seating problems. The models shown here have been expressly designed to meet the needs of both residential and commercial installations and give the highest ultimate performance.

SHELL COLORS
Integral colors Elephant Hide Grey
Beige
Parchment
Lemon Yellow
Sea Foam Green
Bright Red
Applied finish Dark Blue
Mustard
Light Grey
BASE FINISHES Bright Zinc
Black
Birch (rockers in birch only)
Walnut

DAX
Dining and desk chair—the height and angle of the seat are carefully calculated for use at the average desk and dining table.

HT.	W.	D.	SEAT HT.	WT.
31¼"	24⅞"	23½"	17⅞"	14 lb.

DAR
Dining and desk chair—this model has a wire base which is, in fact and feeling, light and strong.

HT.	W.	D.	SEAT HT.	WT.
31½"	24⅞"	24"	17⅞"	10 lb.

SAX
Standard model—a good height and angle for living room, reception room or office—anywhere, in fact, for conversation, reading or relaxing.

HT.	W.	D.	SEAT HT.	WT.
29½"	24⅞"	24½"	16¾"	13 lb.

RAR
Rocking chair—a lightweight rocker ideal for reading, relaxing, and use by the young mother.

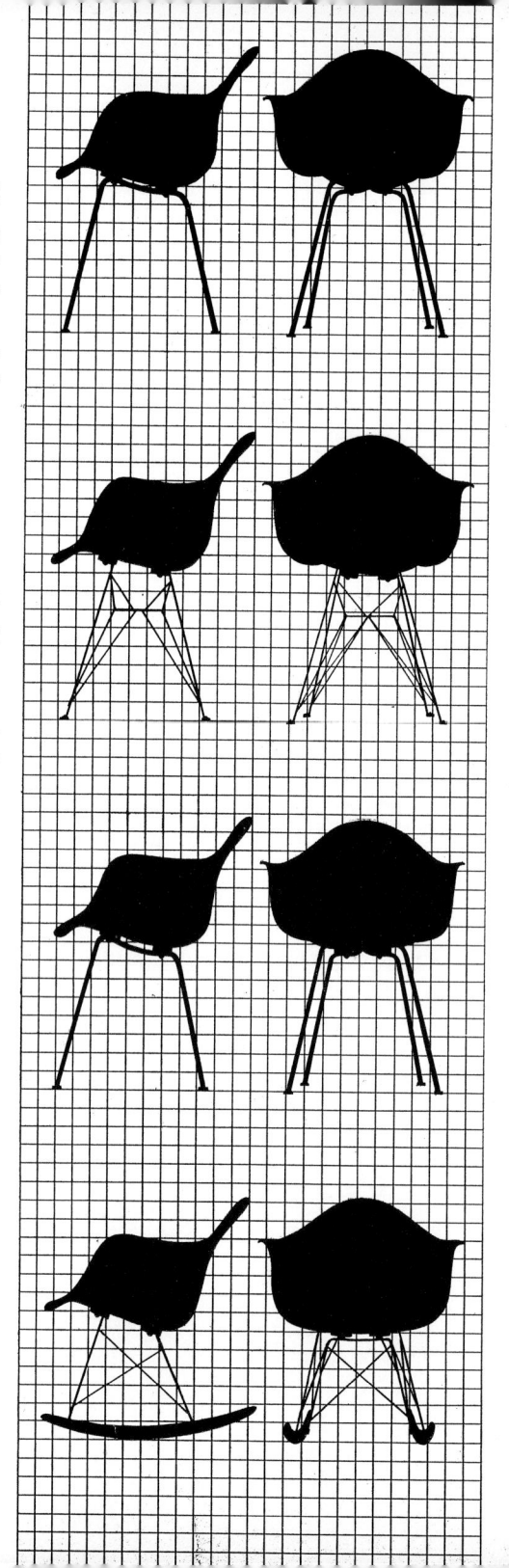

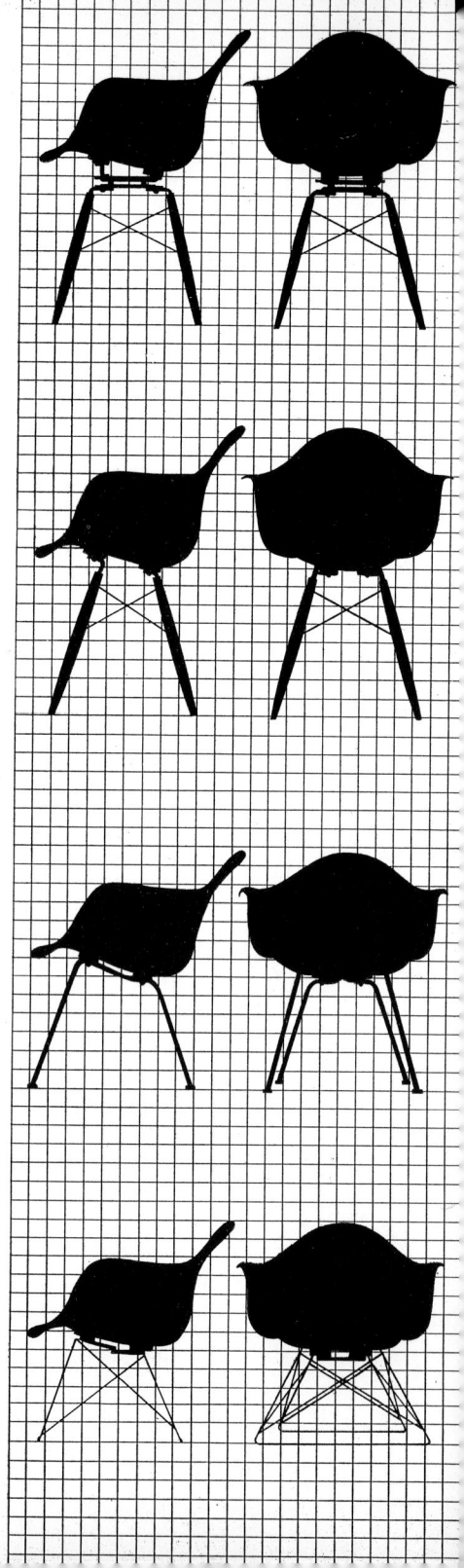

HT.	W.	D.	SEAT HT.	WT.
26⅞"	24⅞"	27"	16"	11 lb.

scale plan views shown on 2" grid
weights shown are net uncrated

PAW

Swivel chair—similar to DAW *except for the addition of a swivel. Excellent for both office and home use.*

HT.	W.	D.	SEAT HT.	WT.
31¼"	24⅞"	24"	17⅞"	12 lb.

DAW

Dining and desk chair—the legs of this model are turned from birch or walnut, with cross bracing of metal.

HT.	W.	D.	SEAT HT.	WT.
31¼"	24⅞"	24"	17⅞"	9 lb.

LAX

Lounge chair—height of seat is lower than that of DAX, *and at an angle that offers restful support. Ideal for reading and relaxed conversation.*

HT.	W.	D.	SEAT HT.	WT.
26⅛"	24⅞"	25⅜"	14⅞"	11 lb.

LAR

Low-low chair — the lowest and lightest of all, perfect for patio, terrace and poolside, for viewing television and for general relaxation.

HT.	W.	D.	SEAT HT.	WT.
24¼"	24⅞"	24½"	12¼"	9 lb.

DAW DAX LAX DAR SAX

LTR

LAR RAR

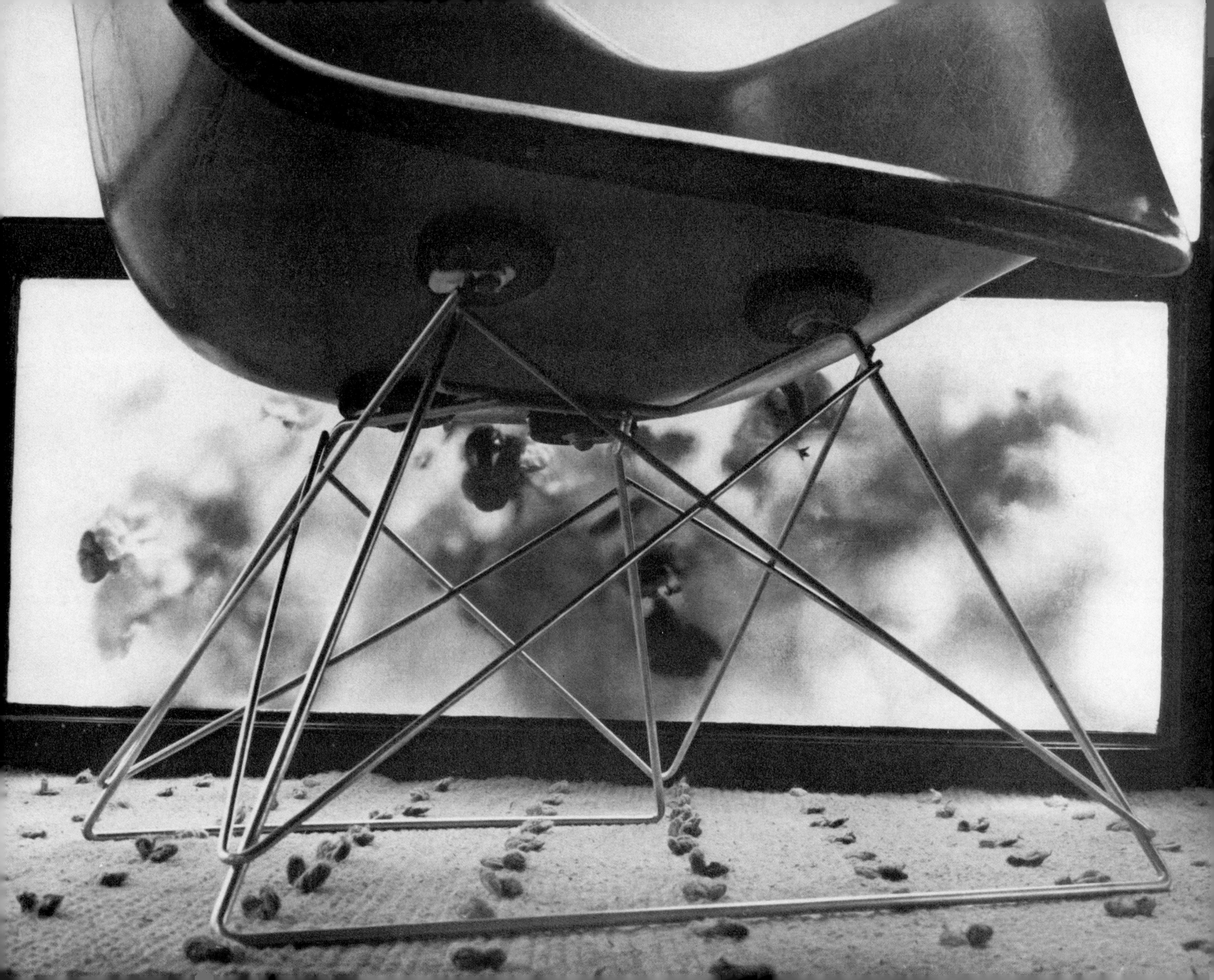

97

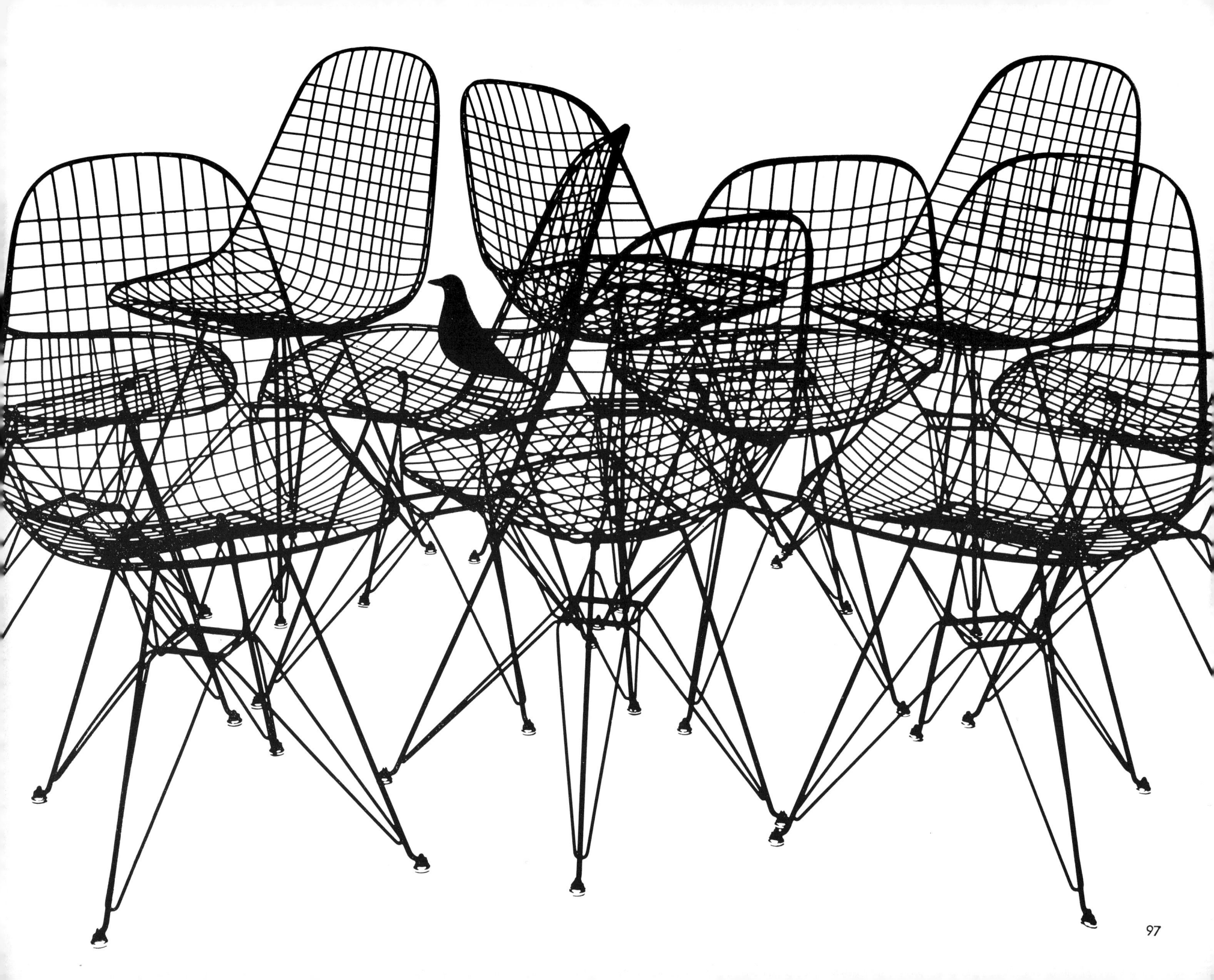

upholstered wire chairs

CONTINUING ITS EFFORTS to produce a comfortable, lightweight and inexpensive chair, Herman Miller has most recently brought out a series of upholstered wire chairs designed by Charles Eames. A welded wire shell, carefully shaped to conform to body contours, supports a resilient cushion that can be easily removed for cleaning or replacement.

The cushion comes in two versions: a single piece foam rubber and hair felt pad, completely covering the wire shell; and a two-piece hair felt pad that covers major portions of the seat and back. Cushions are available in a choice of covers, including exclusive fabrics and genuine leathers.

There are six different bases, both metal and wood, providing models suitable for reading, writing, dining and lounging. The series includes a swivel desk chair and a rocker.

UPHOLSTERY
    Fabrics Pin Check (natural, brown, black)
              Black
    Leather Postman's Bag Tan
BASE FINISHES Natural Birch
                 Walnut

PKW
Desk model—swivel base legs—walnut or birch with cross rod bracing.

HT.	W.	D.	SEAT HT.	WT.
32¾"	19"	21¼"	18½"	14½ lb.

DKW
Dining model — legs — walnut or birch with cross rod bracing.

HT.	W.	D.	SEAT HT.	WT.
32¾"	19"	21¼"	18½"	11 lb.

DKR
Dining model—light base structure of wire rod.

HT.	W.	D.	SEAT HT.	WT
32¾"	19"	21¼"	18½"	12 lb.

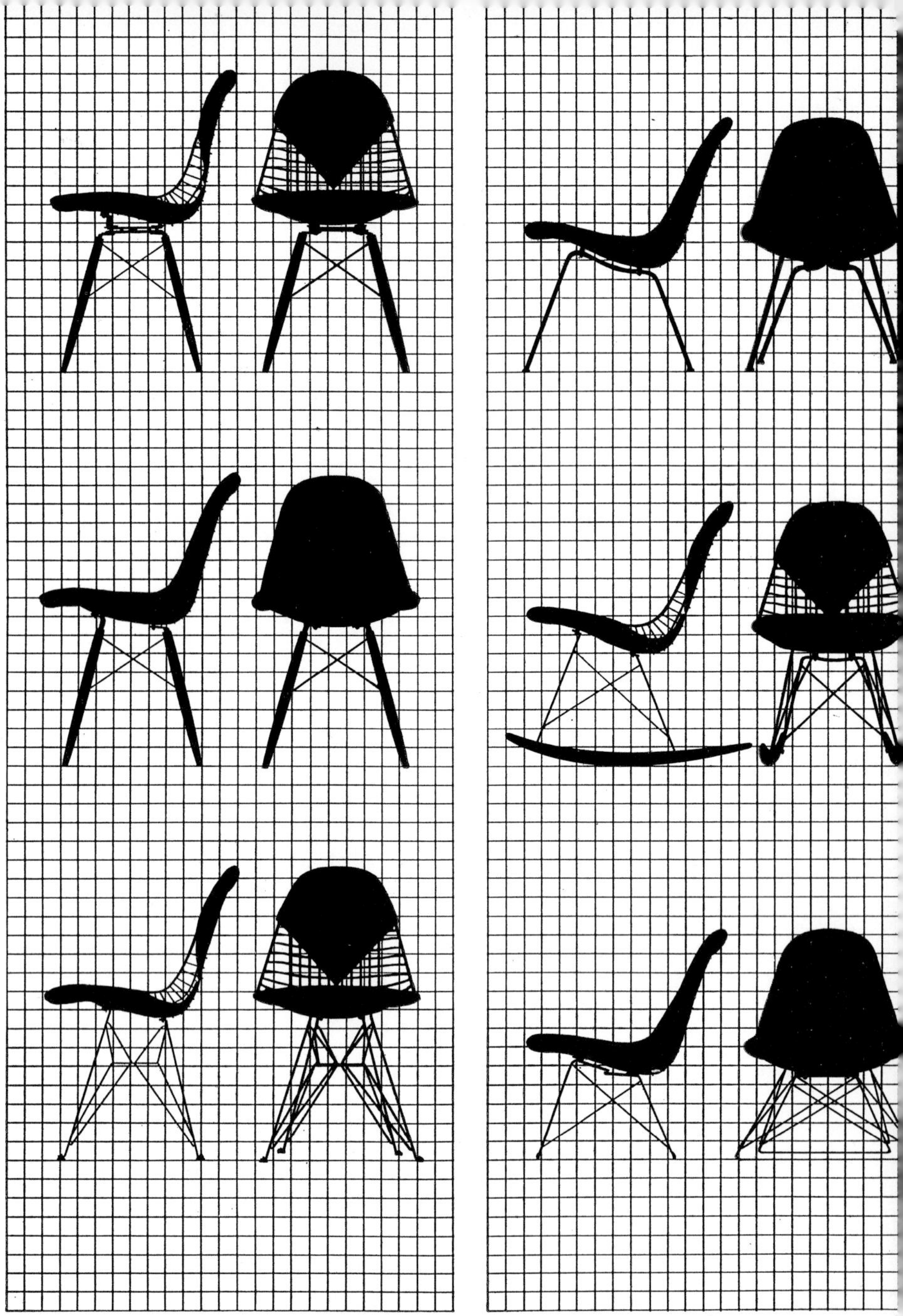

The cushions come in two versions: a single piece pad (add suffix-1 to style no.) and a two piece pad (add suffix-2 to style no.)—both can be easily removed.

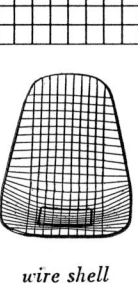

wire shell    *one piece pad*    *two piece pad*    *pad removed*

LKX

Lounge model — cross brace of solid ½" rod.

HT.	W.	D.	SEAT HT.	WT.
27½"	19"	22½"	16"	14½ lb.

RKR

Rocker model — wire rod structure, birch rockers.

HT.	W.	D.	SEAT HT.	WT.
29"	19"	27"	17"	12½ lb.

LKR

Low model — light base structure of wire rod.

HT.	W.	D.	SEAT HT.	WT.
26"	20"	21¾"	13½"	11 lb.

weights shown are net uncrated
scale silhouettes shown on a 2" grid

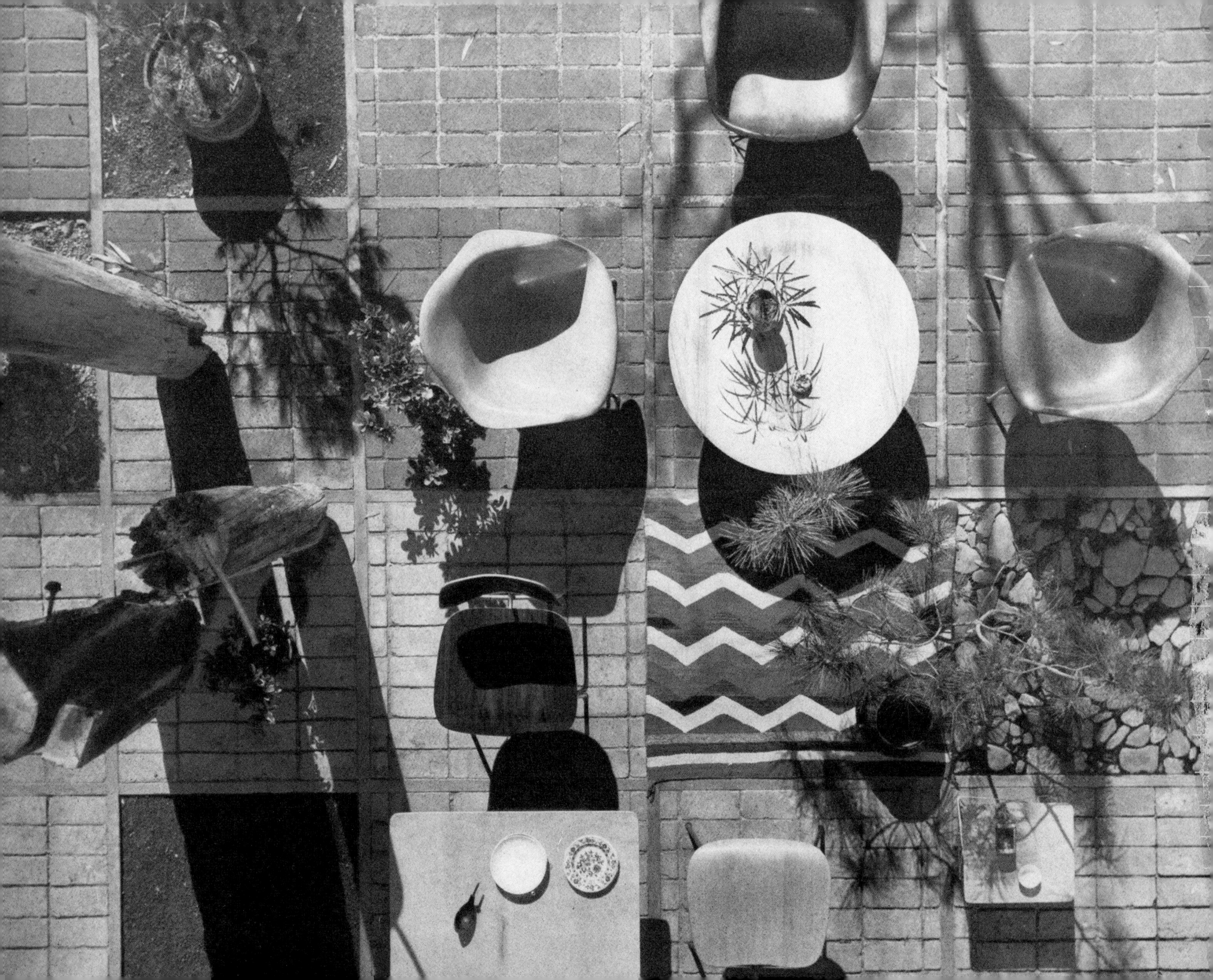

eames storage units

THE EAMES STORAGE UNITS represent a frank and forthright answer to a permanent and basic furniture need: attractive, durable cabinets, cases and desks that are modestly priced. Plated steel uprights support plastic-coated plywood shelves and stain-resistant wood or plastic-coated tops. Crossed metal struts or lacquered masonite panels insure stability. The units come in two widths and three heights, with numerous arrangements including open shelves, sliding panel doors and drawers, in a variety of color combinations. Shown on this page are the standard basic units, while on pages 104 and 105 can be seen the various combinations available.

TOPS AND DRAWERS
(Drawer fronts will match tops)
- Black Plastic Laminate
- Birch
- Walnut

SLIDING DOORS
- Dimpled Wood
- White Glass Cloth Laminate
- Black Hard Plastic

PANELS
(See pg. 104, 105 for standard color combinations)
- Black
- Tan
- Grey
- White
- Red
- Yellow
- Blue

METAL FINISHES
- Bright Zinc
- Black

weights shown are net uncrated
scale silhouettes shown on a 2" grid

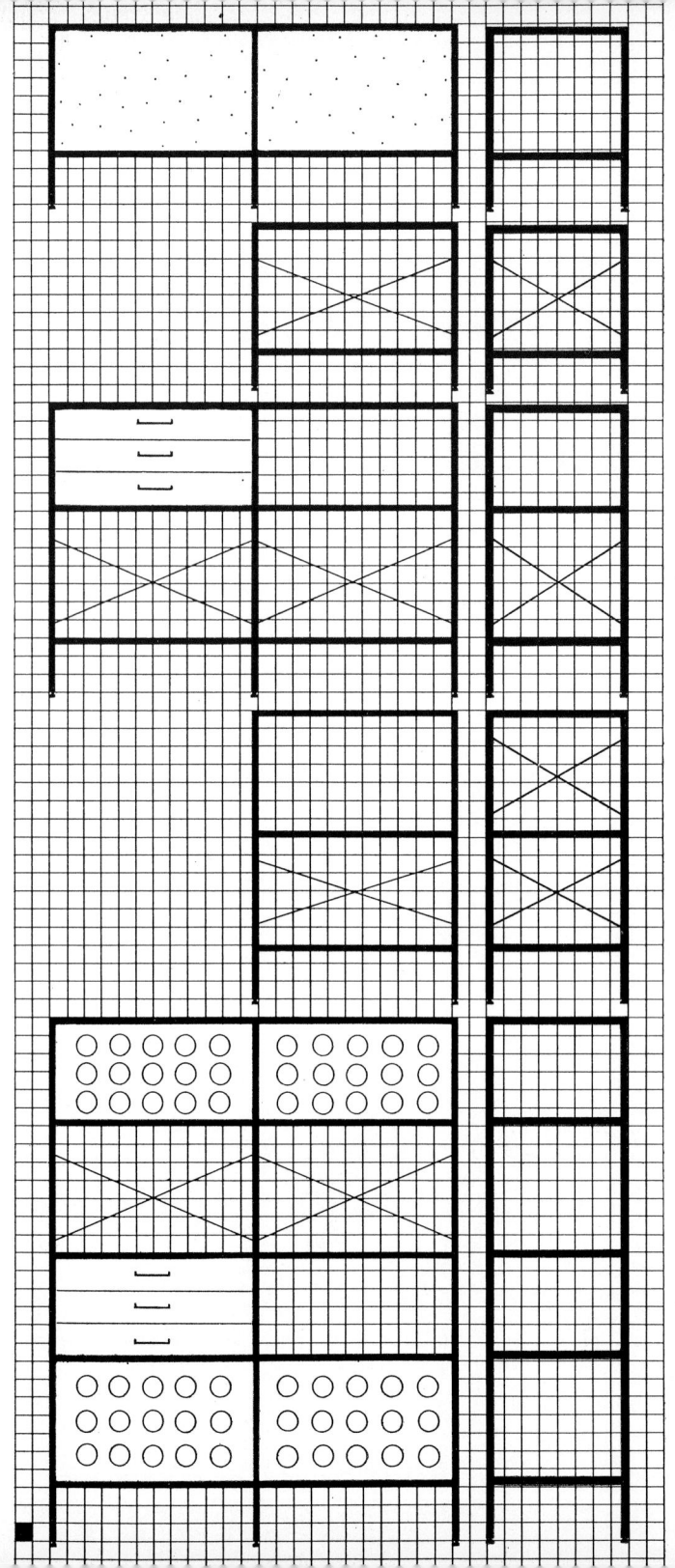

100 series

HT.	W.	D.	WT.
20⅝"	47"	16"	34 lb.

150 series

HT.	W.	D.	WT.
20⅝"	24"	16"	17 lb.

200 series

HT.	W.	D.	WT.
32⅝"	47"	16"	65 lb.

250 series

HT.	W.	D.	WT.
32⅝"	24"	16"	40 lb.

400 series

HT.	W.	D.	WT.
58⅝"	47"	16"	120 lb.

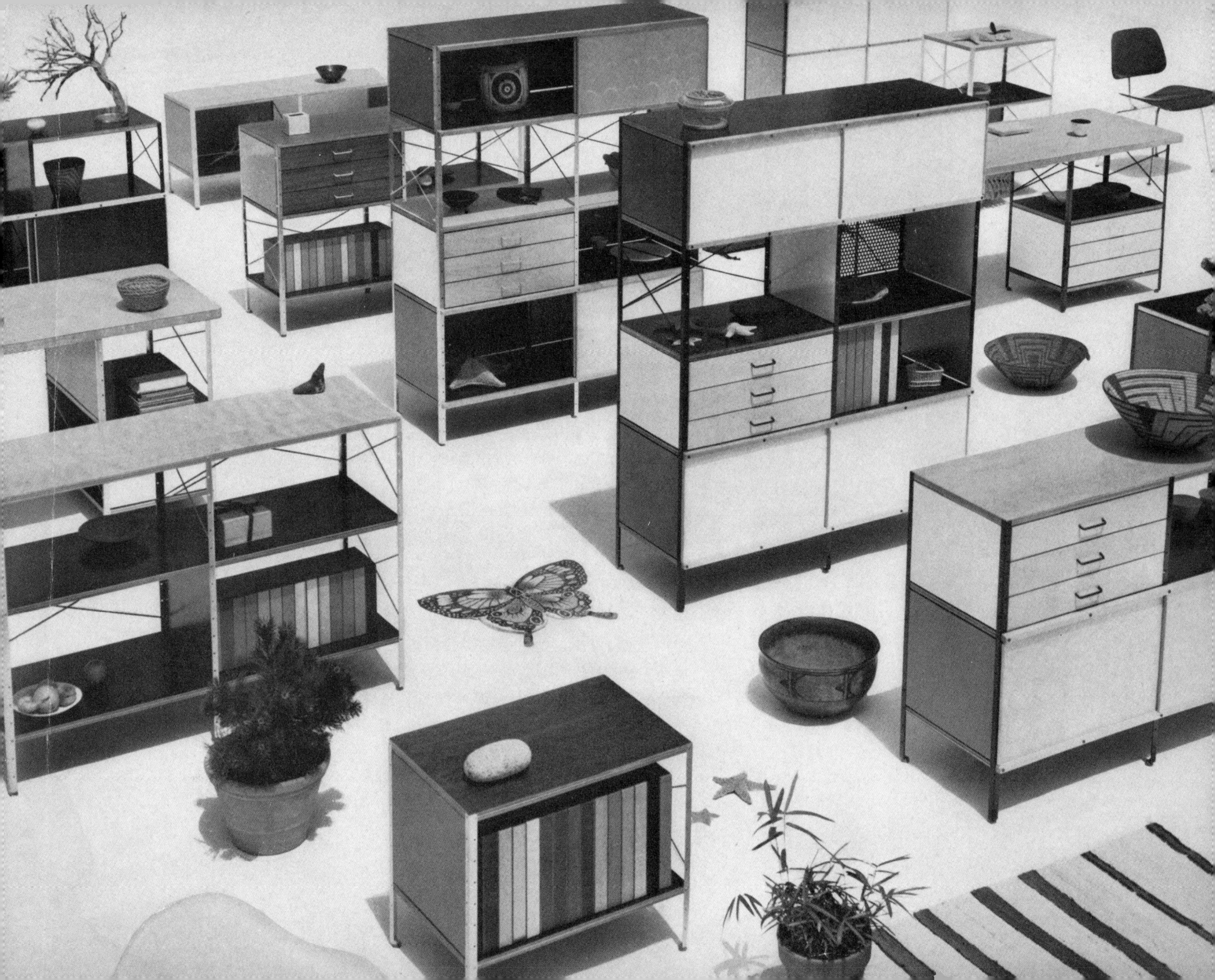

100 series ⟫→

100-C	110-C	150-C
100-N	110-N	150-N

400 series ⟫→

200 series ⤓

These units, being only 20" high, make a pleasing low divider in a room and will fit nicely under windows or for the child's room.

Behind the sliding doors is enclosed storage space that will take 12" albums—especially useful in a room scaled to low dimensions.

There are many uses for this small but versatile open storage unit which is 24 inches wide.

200-C	201-C	210-C	211-C	220-C
200-N	201-N	210-N	211-N	220-N

These are open shelves for open storage—the top shelf will accommodate a 10 inch record album, the bottom will take a 12 inch album.

Of more enclosed construction but for open storage. These shelves hold books or records or the things that accumulate in a playroom.

A three drawer section is in the upper left compartment, the rest of the space for open storage enclosed only by metal cross braces.

With the three drawer section are three open storage compartments, backed by a solid panel, perforated metal grille and metal cross brace.

Three drawers and open storage in two top compartments, the bottom two are enclosed made accessible by a pair of sliding doors

desks ⟫→

D-10-C
Usable from either side

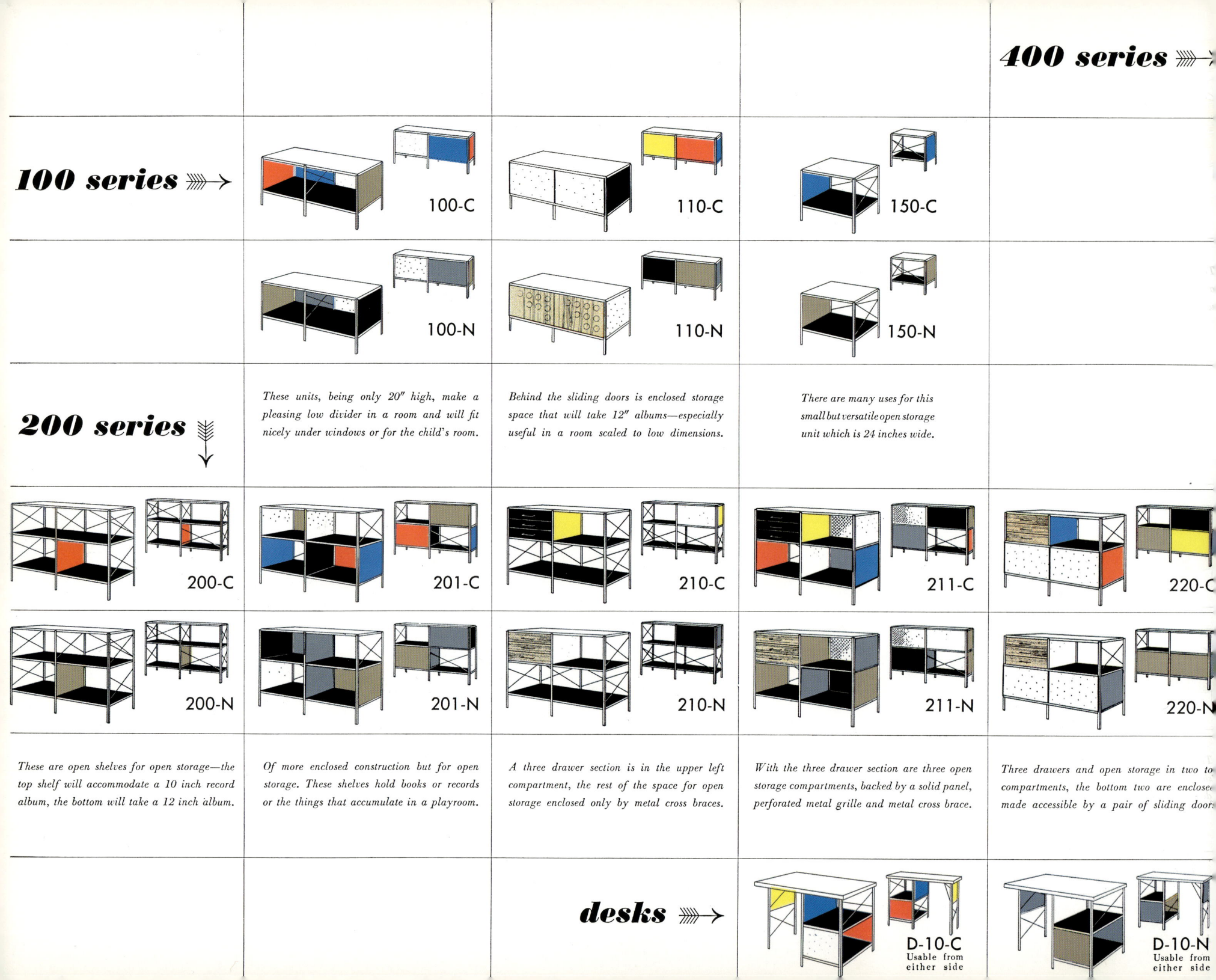

D-10-N
Usable from either side

420-C	**420-N**	**421-C**	**421-N**	**440-K**
These units are 60 inch high and can be used as practical room dividers and in many places where plentiful storage space is required.	The height of the two top shelves are 11¼ and 13¼ inch respectively. The third shelf is 11¼ inch and the bottom shelf is 13¼ inch high.	Sliding doors cover eight lineal feet of storage space. There is also six lineal feet of open shelf and a set of three drawers.	These as well as all other E.S.U. pieces have the same high quality finish on all sides which makes them ideal for use free from wall.	Back and sides completely enclosed by solid panels. The entire front has sliding doors of black and white to form checkerboard pattern.
	240-K	The black and white checkerboard pattern shown on this case can be had in all the other standard units shown on this page.		
230-C	**240-C**	**250-C**	**251-C**	**270-C**
230-N	**240-N**	**250-N**	**251-N**	**270-N**
The top shelf is completely open, the bottom shelf is enclosed with solid panels and sliding doors to provide protected accessible space.	Back and side completely enclosed by solid panels. The entire front has sliding doors— enclosed space for linens, clothes or books.	24 in. versions of the open case serve by themselves and make the system dimensionally fluid.	Also an open storage unit, 24 inches wide, but sides and back have panels and cross braces.	A three drawer section above, open shelves below, cross braces and perforated metal grille.
	D-20-C D-21-C cabinet on left side	**D-20-N** D-21-N cabinet on left side		
Desks to the left have 44"x24½" tops with open storage below for stationery and books. Ideal for the home and school dormitories.			Top dimension is 60"x24½" and 29" in height. Additional uses for the E.S.U. desks as table for sewing or receptionist desk are suggested.	

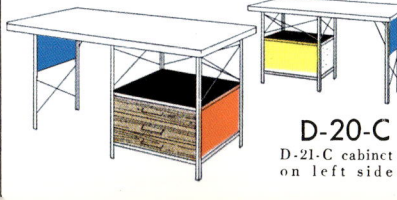

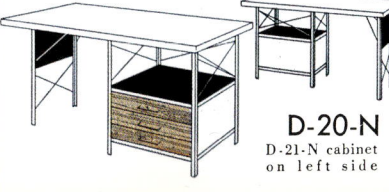

desks

THE E.S.U. COMPONENTS have been combined to make two attractive desks for home or office that are both serviceable and economical. The tops are of the same standard construction as the Eames dining table group, allowing ample space beneath for the average person's legs. Note that both models are available with a file in the lower compartment if desired.

TOP FINISHES	Birch
	Walnut
METAL FINISHES	Bright Zinc
	Black

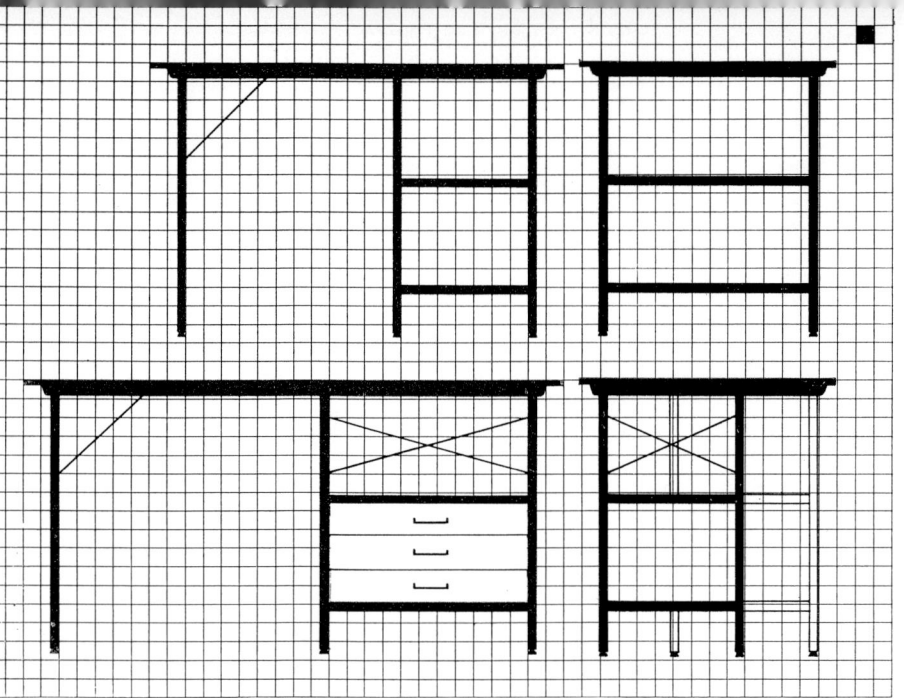

scale silhouettes shown on a 2" grid
weights shown are net uncrated

D-10 series

HT.	W.	D.	WT.
29½"	46"	28"	50 lb.

D-20 series (D-21 reversed)

HT.	W.	D.	WT.
29½"	60"	28"	75 lb.

how to order eames storage units

To place an order for a storage unit, the following information is necessary:

type number　　　　　　　　　　　　　　　　　　　**example: 230-N**

The chart shows the construction type of each unit. Indicate your choice by its code designation. Note that there is a neutral (N) or colorful (C) or black and white (K) finish available in each construction type.

top finish　　　　　　　　　　　　　　　　　　　　**example: BIRCH**

The top shelf is available in black plastic laminate, birch or walnut finish. The drawer fronts in each case will match the top shelf finish. Be sure to stipulate which you wish.

sliding doors　　　　　　　　　　　　　　　　　　**example: DIMPLED**

If the type you wish has sliding doors, these may be obtained in dimpled wood, white glass cloth laminate, or black plastic laminate. Again, note which you wish.

SAMPLE ORDER: 230-N-BIRCH-DIMPLED

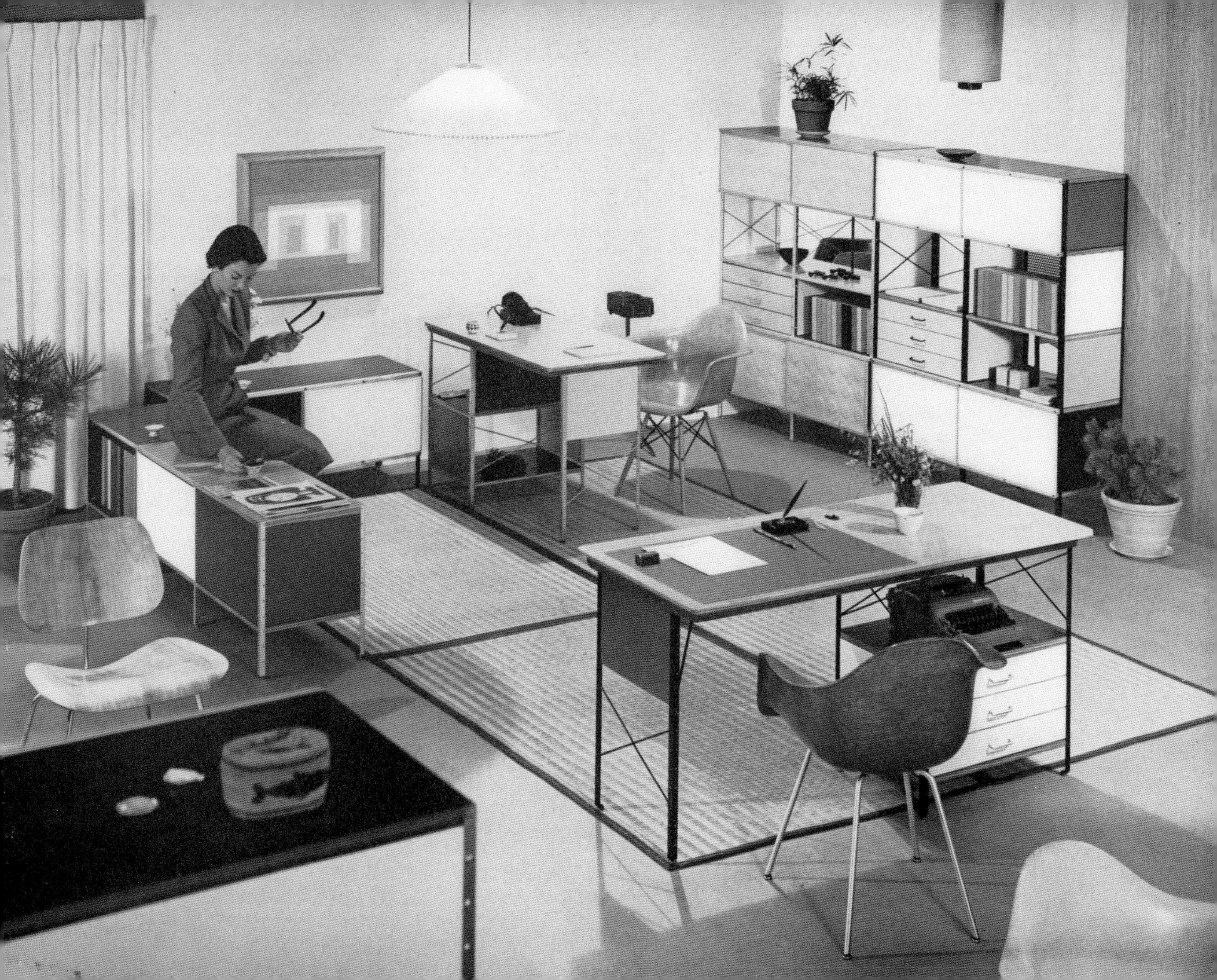

molded plywood folding screens

THE MOLDED PLYWOOD FOLDING SCREEN designed by Charles Eames, offers an excellent solution for problems involving division of areas, screening off objects or activities, or providing backgrounds for furniture groupings. The molded elements fold into each other to form a compact unit when not in use. Their shape enables the screen to stand free open or closed. The plywood surface is decorative yet unobtrusive.

FSW 10

HT.	L.	WT.
5'8"	8'4"	45 lb.

34 FSW 10

HT.	L.	WT.
2'10"	8'4"	23 lb.

FSW 8

HT.	L.	WT.
5'8"	6'8"	36 lb.

34 FSW 8

HT.	L.	WT.
2'10"	6'8"	18 lb.

FSW 6

HT.	L.	WT.
5'8"	5"	27 lb.

34 FSW 6

HT.	L.	WT.
2'10"	5"	14 lb.

WOOD FINISHES Birch
Calico Ash
Oak

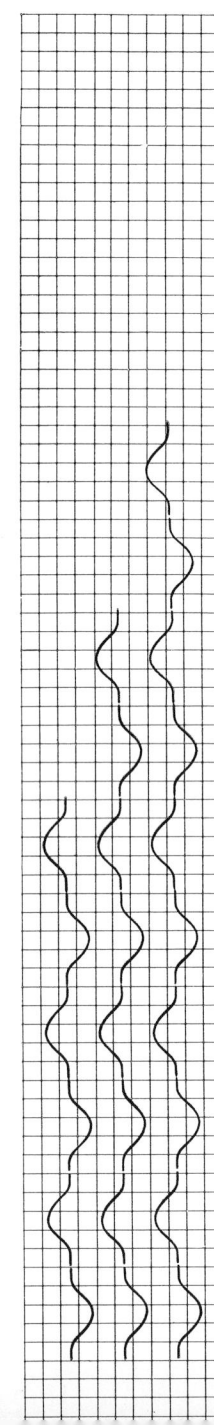

*weights shown are net uncrated
scale plan views shown on 2" grid*

DTM-2 Card table, wood top and folding metal legs. Can be used as dining table extension.

DTW-4 Card table, wood top and wood legs (detachable). Doubles as extension for dining table.

tables

TOP FINISHES
Wood Birch
Ash
Walnut
Oak
Micarta Grey
White

BASE FINISHES
Wood Natural
Birch
Black
Metal Chrome
Black

THESE TABLES ARE AVAILABLE in three sizes, with folding metal legs or detachable wood legs. They can be had with plywood tops, finished with a clear plastic coating which protects the wood from stains and dents, or with tops of Micarta, a hard plastic impervious to stains and scratches. The metal legs, which lock securely in position when in use, can be folded for shipping or storage. The wood legs do not fold but are demountable, facilitating storage and shipping.

| DTM-1 | wood top |
| DTM-10 | micarta top |

Dining table—metal legs fold for storage or shipment.

HT.	L.	W.	WT.
28½"	54"	34"	45 lb.

| DTM-2 | wood top |
| DTM-20 | micarta top |

Card table—folding metal legs. Can be used with dining table.

HT.	L.	W.	WT.
28½"	34"	34"	35 lb.

| IT-1 | wood top |
| IT-10 | micarta top |

Incidental table — metal folding legs. A suitable play table for small children as well as a coffee table or chairside table.

HT.	L.	W.	WT.
17"	21½"	18"	11 lb.

*weights shown are net uncrated
scale silhouettes shown on a 2" grid*

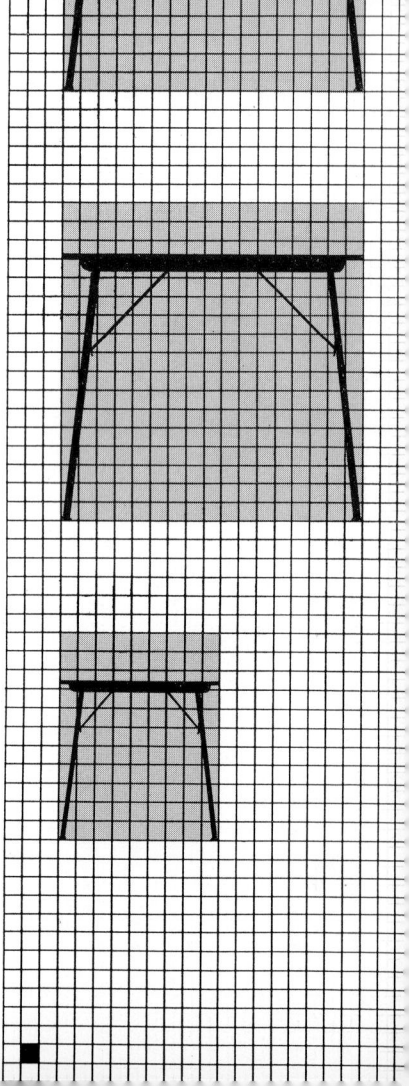

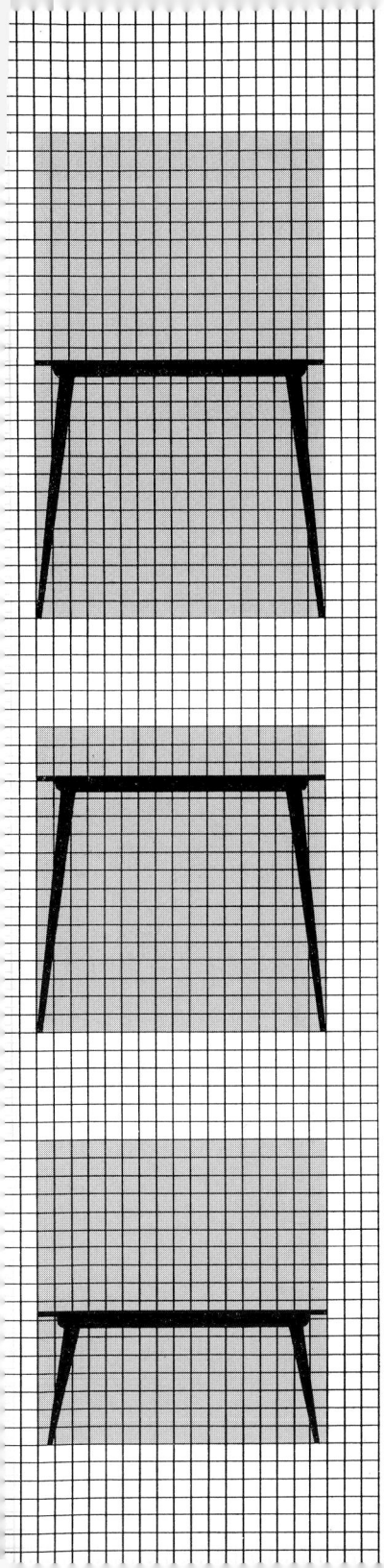

DTW-3   wood top
DTW-30 micarta top

Dining table—wood legs detachable for shipping or storage.

HT.	L.	W.	WT.
28½"	54"	34"	36 lb.

DTW-40 micarta top

Card table—wood legs detachable. Can be used with dining table.

HT.	L.	W.	WT.
28½"	34"	34"	29 lb.

DTW-2 and plywood chairs shown as breakfast group. ⇛→

DTW-50 micarta top

Coffee table—detachable wood legs. Top is same size as card table.

HT.	L.	W.	WT.
15"	34"	34"	27 lb.

DAX   DTM-1   LCM   DTM-2

DTW-50

DTW-3

DCM

IT-10

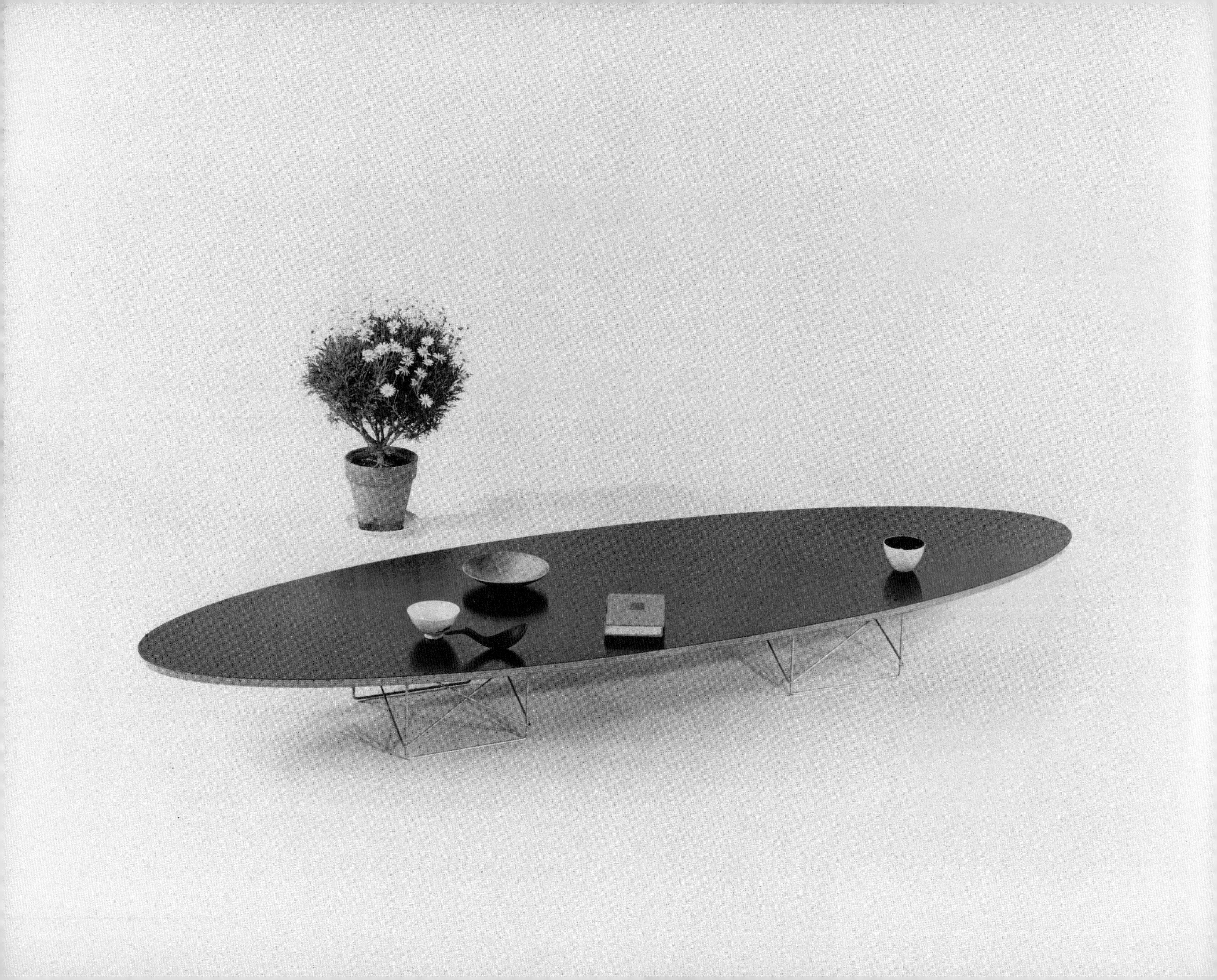

scale silhouettes shown on 2" grid
weights shown are net uncrated

ETR

A long, low coffee table with a black laminated plastic top and wire strut base.

HT.	L.	W.	WT.
10"	89¼"	29⅜"	45 lb.

LTR

Occasional table with wire strut base which can double as stool. Small, light, strong and handy. Also a child's play table.

HT.	L.	W.	WT.
10"	15⅝"	13⅜"	5 lb.

CTW

Round coffee table with molded plywood top and molded plywood legs.

HT.	DIA.	WT.
15½"	34"	10 lb.

CTM

Round coffee table with molded plywood top and metal legs.

HT.	DIA.	WT.
15½"	34"	18 lb.

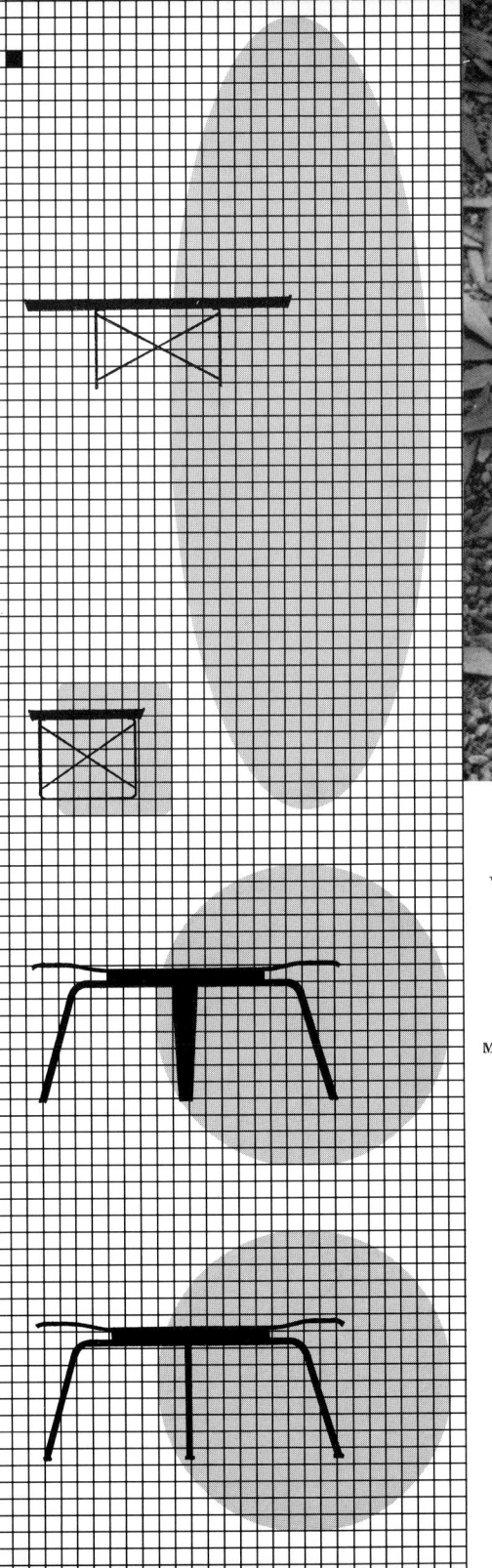

WOOD FINISHES Birch, Walnut, Ash, Oak, Black, Red

METAL FINISHES Chrome, Black

LTR
TOP FINISHES Black, Birch, Walnut
BASE FINISHES Bright Zinc, Black

CTW
WOOD FINISHES Birch, Walnut, Ash, Oak, Black, Red

CTM

PRINTING	*J. W. Field.*
PHOTOGRAPHY	*Majority of photographs by Dale Rooks, with supplementary pictures by Ezra Stoller, Midori and William Vandivert. Photos of Charles Eames section by Charles Eames office.*
DESIGN	*George Nelson. Organization of material and layout by Ernest Farmer. Charles Eames section by Charles and Ray Eames. Organization of material and layout by Charles Kratka. Dust jacket by Irving Harper.*

Printed in the United States of America.